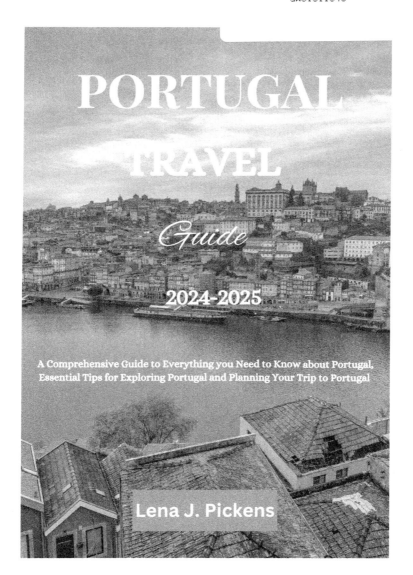

Copyright © by Lena J. Pickens 2024. All rights reserved.

Before this document is duplicated or reproduced in any manner, the publisher's consent must be gained.

Therefore, the contents within can neither be stored electronically, transferred, nor kept in a database. Neither in part nor full can the document be copied, scanned, faxed, or retained without approval from the publisher.

Table of Contents

Cover

Portugal Images

1. INTRODUCTION TO PORTUGAL

- Discovering the Charm of Portugal

- Geography and Climate

- History and Culture

2. PLANNING YOUR TRIP

- Best Time to Visit

- Visa Requirements and Entry Information

- Budgeting and Money Matters

- Travel Insurance and Health Tips

3. GETTING TO KNOW PORTUGAL

- Regions and Cities Overview

- Lisbon: Portugal's Vibrant Capital

- Porto: City of Bridges and Port Wine

- The Algarve: Stunning Coastline and Beaches

- Coimbra: Historical University Town

- Sintra: Fairytale Palaces and Gardens

- Douro Valley: Wine Country and River Cruises

4. TOP ATTRACTIONS AND LANDMARKS

- UNESCO World Heritage Sites

- Castles, Palaces, and Fortresses

- Natural Parks and Scenic Landscapes

- Beaches and Coastal Towns

5. EXPERIENCING PORTUGUESE CULTURE

- Fado Music and Traditional Performances

- Culinary Delights: Port Wine, Pastries, and Seafood

- Festivals and Celebrations

- Art, Architecture, and Handicrafts

6. OUTDOOR ADVENTURES

- Hiking and Trekking Routes

- Surfing and Water Sports

- Cycling Tours and Trails

- Golfing in Portugal

7. EATING AND DRINKING IN PORTUGAL

- Dining spots

- Best dishes

8. PRACTICAL INFORMATION

- Accommodation Options: Hotels, Pousadas, and Guesthouses

- Dining and Nightlife Recommendations

- Transportation: Getting Around by Train, Bus, and Car

- Safety Tips and Emergency Contacts

9. DAY TRIPS AND EXCURSIONS

- Discovering nearby Islands and Towns

- Wine Tasting Tours and Vineyard Visits

- Cultural Tours and Local Experiences

10. LANGUAGE AND COMMUNICATION

- Useful Portuguese Phrases and Expressions

- Etiquette and Cultural Norms

11. SHOPPING GUIDE

- Souvenirs and Local Products

- Markets and Shopping Districts

Chapter 1

Introduction to Portugal

Nestled on the western edge of the Iberian Peninsula, Portugal is a country rich in history, culture, and natural beauty. From its picturesque coastal villages to its vibrant cities, Portugal offers a diverse array of experiences for travelers and residents alike.

As one of the oldest nations in Europe, Portugal's history is steeped in tradition and exploration. From the early seafaring adventures of explorers like Vasco da Gama and Ferdinand Magellan to the heights of the Age of Discovery, Portugal played a significant role in shaping the course of world history. This legacy is evident in its architecture, cuisine, and cultural heritage.

Today, Portugal is known for its warm climate, stunning beaches, and welcoming atmosphere. The country boasts a unique blend of influences, from its Moorish past to its maritime connections with Africa, Asia, and the Americas. Visitors can explore medieval castles, sample delicious wines in the Douro Valley, or simply relax on the sun-drenched shores of the Algarve.

In addition to its natural beauty, Portugal is also home to a thriving arts and culinary scene. Lisbon, the capital city, is a vibrant hub of culture, with its winding streets, colorful neighborhoods, and lively nightlife. From traditional fado music to cutting-edge contemporary art, there's something for everyone to enjoy.

Portugal's cuisine is a reflection of its diverse history and geography. From fresh seafood dishes to hearty stews, Portuguese cuisine is rich in flavor and variety. Don't miss the opportunity to try iconic dishes like bacalhau (salted cod), pastéis de nata (custard tarts), and grilled sardines.

Whether you're exploring its historic cities, relaxing on its beautiful beaches, or savoring its delicious cuisine, Portugal offers a truly unforgettable experience. With its welcoming people, rich culture, and breathtaking landscapes, it's no wonder that Portugal continues to capture the hearts of travelers from around the world

Discovering the Charm of Portugal

Portugal, with its captivating blend of old-world charm and modern allure, beckons travelers to uncover its hidden treasures. From the cobbled streets of historic towns to the rugged cliffs of the Atlantic coast, Portugal offers a tapestry of experiences that enchant visitors at every turn.

One of the most alluring aspects of Portugal is its rich history, evident in its well-preserved architecture and cultural landmarks. Wander through the narrow alleys of Lisbon's Alfama district, where the echoes of centuries past linger in the air. Marvel at the grandeur of Porto's historic Ribeira district, lined with colorful buildings that overlook the Douro River. Explore the ancient university town of Coimbra, where medieval streets lead to magnificent palaces and libraries.

Beyond its cities, Portugal's countryside is a treasure trove of natural beauty. The Douro Valley, with its terraced vineyards and meandering river, is a UNESCO World Heritage Site renowned for its wine production and scenic splendor. The rugged coastline of the Algarve, dotted with hidden coves and sandy beaches, invites travelers to unwind and soak in the sun.

Portugal's charm also lies in its vibrant culture and warm hospitality. Experience the soul-stirring melodies of fado music in a cozy tavern, where the haunting vocals and plaintive guitar evoke a sense of longing and nostalgia. Savor the flavors of Portuguese cuisine, from hearty seafood stews to delicate pastries, each dish a testament to the country's culinary heritage.

For those seeking adventure, Portugal offers a wealth of outdoor activities, from hiking in the lush forests of Sintra to surfing along the Atlantic coast. Embark on a boat tour of the breathtaking Azores archipelago, where volcanic landscapes and azure waters create a paradise for nature lovers.

But perhaps the true charm of Portugal lies in its people, whose warmth and hospitality make visitors feel like cherished guests. Whether sharing stories over a glass of port wine or joining in a traditional festival, the Portuguese welcome travelers with open arms and a genuine sense of camaraderie.

In every corner of Portugal, there is a story waiting to be discovered, a landscape waiting to be explored, and a moment waiting to be savored. With its timeless allure and endless delights, Portugal invites travelers to embark on a journey of discovery and fall under its spell.

Geography and Climate

Nestled in the southwestern corner of Europe, Portugal boasts a diverse geography and a mild Mediterranean climate that has long drawn visitors to its shores. From verdant mountains to golden beaches, Portugal's landscape is as varied as it is breathtaking.

Geographically, Portugal is characterized by its three main regions: the mainland, the Azores archipelago, and the

Madeira islands. The mainland is divided into several distinct zones, including the fertile plains of the north, the rugged mountains of the interior, and the sun-drenched coastlines of the south.

In the north, the landscape is dominated by the rolling hills of the Minho and Trás-os-Montes regions, where lush greenery and vineyards thrive in the temperate climate. Further south, the terrain becomes more mountainous, with the Serra da Estrela range rising to over 1,900 meters (6,200 feet) and offering opportunities for skiing in the winter months.

Along the coast, Portugal's beaches are renowned for their beauty and variety. From the dramatic cliffs of the Algarve to the secluded coves of the Costa Vicentina, there is a beach to suit every taste. In addition to its mainland coastline, Portugal is also home to the Azores and Madeira, two island chains in the Atlantic Ocean known for their volcanic landscapes, lush vegetation, and stunning natural beauty.

Portugal's climate is influenced by its proximity to the Atlantic Ocean, resulting in mild winters and warm summers. In general, the northern and central regions of Portugal experience a temperate maritime climate, with cool, wet winters and hot, dry summers. The southern region, including the Algarve, enjoys a Mediterranean climate characterized by mild, wet winters and hot, dry summers.

One of the most notable features of Portugal's climate is its sunshine. With over 300 days of sunshine per year in many areas, Portugal is one of the sunniest countries in Europe, making it an ideal destination for outdoor activities year-round.

Despite its relatively small size, Portugal's diverse geography and climate offer a wealth of opportunities for outdoor exploration and adventure. Whether hiking in the mountains, surfing along the coast, or simply relaxing on the beach, Portugal invites visitors to immerse themselves in its natural splendor and enjoy its Mediterranean charm.

History and Culture of Portugal

With a rich tapestry of historical events and cultural influences, Portugal's story is as captivating as it is diverse. From its early beginnings as a Celtic settlement to its rise as a global maritime power, Portugal's history has shaped its unique identity and cultural heritage.

Early History:
Portugal's history dates back thousands of years, with evidence of human settlement dating back to the Paleolithic era. In ancient times, the region was inhabited by various

tribes, including the Celts, Phoenicians, and Romans, each leaving their mark on the land.

The Moorish Period:
In the 8th century, the Moors invaded the Iberian Peninsula, bringing with them Islamic culture and architecture. For centuries, Portugal was under Moorish rule, until the Christian Reconquista began in the 11th century, leading to the gradual reconquest of the region by Christian forces.

The Age of Discovery:
Portugal's golden age began in the 15th century with the Age of Discovery, a period of exploration and expansion that would shape the course of world history. Led by daring navigators such as Vasco da Gama and Ferdinand Magellan, Portuguese explorers ventured into uncharted waters, establishing trade routes to Africa, Asia, and the Americas. This era of exploration brought wealth and prestige to

Portugal, as well as a rich cultural exchange that left an indelible mark on its art, architecture, and cuisine.

The Age of Empire:

By the 16th century, Portugal had become a global maritime empire, with colonies stretching from Brazil to India. Lisbon, the capital city, flourished as a center of commerce and culture, attracting merchants, scholars, and artists from around the world. This period of prosperity saw the construction of magnificent palaces, churches, and monasteries, many of which still stand as a testament to Portugal's imperial past.

Decline and Revival:

Despite its golden age, Portugal's empire eventually began to decline, as rival powers such as Spain, England, and the Netherlands challenged its dominance. In the 18th century, Portugal suffered a devastating earthquake and tsunami that destroyed much of Lisbon and plunged the country into economic hardship. However, Portugal would eventually recover, thanks in part to the discovery of gold in Brazil and the establishment of new trading partners in Asia.

Modern Portugal:

In the 20th century, Portugal underwent significant political upheaval, including the fall of the monarchy, the establishment of a republic, and a period of dictatorship under António de Oliveira Salazar. In 1974, a peaceful revolution known as the Carnation Revolution brought an end to the dictatorship and paved the way for democracy.

Today, Portugal is a vibrant and cosmopolitan nation, known for its warm hospitality, rich cultural heritage, and stunning natural beauty. From the charming streets of Lisbon to the sun-drenched beaches of the Algarve, Portugal continues to captivate visitors with its history, culture, and timeless allure.

Chapter 2

Planning Your Trip

Planning a trip to Portugal offers a plethora of options for travelers seeking history, culture, natural beauty, and adventure. Whether you're drawn to the bustling streets of Lisbon, the tranquil vineyards of the Douro Valley, or the sun-kissed beaches of the Algarve, careful planning can help you make the most of your Portuguese adventure.

1. Choosing Your Destinations:

- Start by deciding which regions of Portugal you want to explore. Lisbon and Porto are popular choices for their vibrant city life and historical significance, while the Algarve beckons with its stunning coastline.

- Consider whether you want to focus on urban exploration, outdoor activities, cultural immersion, or a mix of everything. Portugal offers something for every traveler's preferences.

2. Setting Your Itinerary:

- Determine the duration of your trip and allocate time for each destination accordingly. Keep in mind transportation times between cities and regions.
- Prioritize must-see attractions and experiences, but also leave room for spontaneity and relaxation. Portugal's laid-back atmosphere encourages leisurely exploration.

3. Accommodation:

- Research and book accommodation well in advance, especially during peak travel seasons. Options range from boutique hotels and guesthouses to apartments and hostels.
- Consider staying in different types of accommodations to enhance your experience. For example, opt for a historic

pousada (traditional inn) or a countryside villa for a unique stay.

4. Transportation:

- Decide on the most suitable mode of transportation for your itinerary. Portugal has an extensive network of trains, buses, and highways, making it easy to travel between cities and regions.

- Renting a car offers flexibility and the opportunity to explore off-the-beaten-path destinations, but be prepared for narrow roads and parking challenges in urban areas.

5. Activities and Experiences:

- Research local activities and experiences that align with your interests. Whether it's wine tasting in the Douro Valley, surfing in Nazaré, or exploring historic castles in Sintra, Portugal offers a wide range of options.

- Consider guided tours or excursions to gain deeper insights into Portugal's history, culture, and natural wonders. Local guides can provide valuable expertise and insider tips.

6. Cuisine and Dining:

  - Explore Portugal's culinary scene by sampling traditional dishes, seafood specialties, and regional delicacies. Don't miss the opportunity to indulge in pastéis de nata (custard tarts) and fresh seafood.

  - Venture beyond tourist areas to discover authentic local restaurants and markets where you can savor the flavors of Portuguese cuisine.

7. Cultural Etiquette:

  - Familiarize yourself with Portuguese customs and etiquette to ensure a smooth and respectful travel experience. Greetings, dining etiquette, and tipping practices may vary from what you're accustomed to.

  - Embrace the laid-back pace of Portuguese life and be open to engaging with locals. A few basic phrases in

Portuguese can go a long way in fostering connections and showing appreciation.

8. Safety and Health:

- Take necessary precautions to ensure your safety while traveling in Portugal. Keep important documents secure, be aware of your surroundings, and follow local laws and regulations.

- Consider travel insurance that covers medical emergencies and trip cancellations. Familiarize yourself with healthcare facilities and emergency services in the areas you'll be visiting.

By carefully planning your trip to Portugal, you can create unforgettable memories and immerse yourself in the rich culture, history, and natural beauty that this enchanting country has to offer. Whether you're exploring ancient landmarks, savoring delicious cuisine, or simply soaking up the sun on a picturesque beach, Portugal is sure to captivate your heart and inspire your spirit of adventure.

Best Time to Visit

Choosing the best time to visit Portugal depends on your preferences for weather, crowds, and activities. Portugal enjoys a Mediterranean climate with mild winters and hot summers, making it a year-round destination. However, each season offers unique experiences and advantages. Here's a breakdown of what to expect during different times of the year:

Spring (March to May)

Pros:

- Mild Weather: Spring brings pleasant temperatures, typically ranging from 15°C to 25°C (59°F to 77°F), making it ideal for sightseeing and outdoor activities.

- Blooming Landscapes: The countryside is lush and vibrant, with wildflowers in full bloom, especially in regions like the Douro Valley and Alentejo.
- Fewer Crowds: Tourist crowds are lighter compared to the summer months, providing a more relaxed experience at popular attractions.

Activities:

- Exploring historical sites and cultural landmarks.
- Wine-tasting tours in the Douro Valley.
- Hiking and nature walk in national parks.

Summer (June to August)

Pros:

- Beach Weather: Summer is perfect for beach lovers, with temperatures ranging from 20°C to 30°C (68°F to 86°F) and plenty of sunshine.

- Festivals: Numerous festivals take place, including Lisbon's Festa de Santo António in June and Porto's Festa de São João.

Cons:

- Crowds: This is peak tourist season, so expect larger crowds at popular destinations and higher prices for accommodation.
- Heat: Inland areas can get very hot, sometimes exceeding 35°C (95°F).

Activities:

- Relaxing on the beaches of the Algarve and Costa Vicentina.
- Attending local festivals and cultural events.
- Exploring coastal towns and enjoying water sports.

Autumn (September to November)

Pros:

- Pleasant Temperatures: Autumn offers comfortable temperatures, usually between 15°C and 25°C (59°F to 77°F), ideal for outdoor activities.
- Harvest Season: This is a great time for food and wine enthusiasts, as it coincides with the grape harvest in the wine regions.
- Reduced Crowds: The summer crowds have dissipated, making it easier to explore at a leisurely pace.

Activities:

- Participating in wine harvest and tasting tours.
- Exploring historic cities like Lisbon, Porto, and Sintra.
- Hiking and cycling in cooler weather.

Winter (December to February)

Pros:

- Mild Winters: Coastal areas, including Lisbon and the Algarve, experience mild winters with temperatures ranging from 8°C to 15°C (46°F to 59°F).
- Lower Prices: Winter is the off-peak season, so you can find better deals on flights and accommodations.
- Fewer Tourists: Attractions are less crowded, providing a more intimate experience.

Cons:

- Cooler Temperatures: While coastal areas remain mild, inland regions and northern Portugal can be quite cold, especially at higher altitudes.

Activities:

- Exploring cities and cultural sites without the crowds.
- Enjoying local cuisine in cozy restaurants.
- Visiting Christmas markets and winter festivals.

Special Considerations:

- Azores and Madeira: These island regions have a more temperate climate year-round, making them excellent destinations at any time. Spring and autumn are particularly good for avoiding the high summer humidity.

- Events and Festivals: Check the local event calendar as Portugal hosts numerous festivals throughout the year, which can enhance your travel experience.

In summary, the best time to visit Portugal depends on your personal preferences and what you want to experience. Whether you're looking for beach vacations, cultural exploration, or culinary delights, Portugal offers something special in every season.

Visa Requirements and Entry Information for Portugal

Portugal, as a member of the European Union (EU) and part of the Schengen Area, has specific visa requirements and entry rules that vary depending on your nationality and the purpose of your visit. Understanding these requirements is essential for a smooth travel experience.

Schengen Area

Portugal is part of the Schengen Area, a group of 27 European countries that have abolished passport control at their mutual borders. A Schengen visa allows for travel within the entire Schengen Zone for up to 90 days within a 180-day period.

Who Needs a Visa?

EU/EEA/Swiss Citizens:

- Citizens of the European Union (EU), European Economic Area (EEA), and Switzerland do not need a visa to enter Portugal. They can stay, work, and live in Portugal without any time restrictions.

Non-EU/EEA Citizens:

- Visa-Exempt Countries: Citizens of certain countries, including the United States, Canada, Australia, New Zealand, Japan, and many others, can enter Portugal for tourism or business purposes without a visa for up to 90 days within a 180-day period.
- Visa-Required Countries: Citizens of countries not on the visa-exempt list must obtain a Schengen visa before traveling to Portugal. This visa allows for stays of up to 90 days within a 180-day period for tourism, business, or family visits.

Types of Visas

1. Short-Stay Schengen Visa (Type C):

   - Tourist Visa: For leisure travel, sightseeing, and visiting friends or family.

- Business Visa: For business meetings, conferences, and professional purposes.

- Cultural/Sports Visa: For participating in cultural or sports events.

2. Long-Stay National Visa (Type D):

- For stays longer than 90 days, such as for work, study, or family reunification. Applicants must apply for this visa specific to Portugal.

How to Apply for a Schengen Visa

1. Determine Where to Apply:

- If Portugal is your main destination (where you will spend the most time), you should apply for a visa at the Portuguese consulate or embassy in your home country.

- If traveling to multiple Schengen countries, apply at the consulate of the country where you will spend the most time or where you first enter the Schengen Zone.

2. Gather Required Documents:

- Completed visa application form.

- Valid passport (with at least two blank pages and valid for at least three months beyond your planned departure date from the Schengen Area).

- Recent passport-sized photos.

- Proof of travel insurance covering medical expenses and emergencies (minimum coverage of €30,000).

- Proof of accommodation (hotel bookings, invitation letter from a host).

- Proof of sufficient financial means (bank statements, pay slips).

- Flight itinerary or reservation.

- Purpose of visit documentation (e.g., invitation letter, conference registration).

3. Schedule an Appointment:

   - Schedule an appointment at the Portuguese consulate or visa application center in your country.

4. Attend the Visa Interview:

   - Attend your appointment with all required documents and be prepared to answer questions about your travel plans.

5. Pay the Visa Fee:

   - The visa fee is typically around €80 for adults, with reduced rates for children and certain categories of applicants.

6. Wait for Processing:

- Visa processing times vary but generally take about 15 calendar days. It's advisable to apply well in advance of your travel date.

Entry Requirements

Upon arrival in Portugal, you will need to present:

- A valid passport or EU national ID card.

- A valid visa if required (for non-exempt travelers).

- Proof of onward or return travel.

- Proof of sufficient funds for your stay.

- Travel insurance (if applicable).

Additional Considerations

- Extended Stays: If you plan to stay in Portugal for more than 90 days, you will need to apply for a residence permit or long-stay visa appropriate to your situation (e.g., work, study, family reunion).

- Border Controls: While border checks within the Schengen Area are minimal, always carry your passport or ID card when traveling between countries.
- Health Regulations: Be aware of any health and vaccination requirements, especially in light of global health concerns.

By understanding and preparing for the visa requirements and entry information, you can ensure a smooth and enjoyable visit to Portugal.

Budgeting and Money Matters

Planning a trip to Portugal involves careful budgeting and understanding the local financial landscape to make the most of your visit. Here's a comprehensive guide to help you manage your finances efficiently while traveling in Portugal.

Currency and Exchange Rates

Currency:

- Portugal uses the Euro (€), abbreviated as EUR.

- Coins come in denominations of 1, 2, 5, 10, 20, and 50 cents, and €1 and €2.

- Banknotes are available in €5, €10, €20, €50, €100, €200, and €500, though €200 and €500 notes are rarely used in everyday transactions.

Exchange Rates:

- Exchange rates fluctuate, so check the current rate before you travel. As of 2024, €1 is roughly equivalent to $1.10 USD, but this can vary.

Currency Exchange:

- Currency can be exchanged at banks, exchange bureaus, airports, and major hotels.
- Avoid exchanging large amounts at airports due to higher fees and less favorable rates.
- ATMs (locally known as "Multibanco") offer competitive exchange rates and are widely available.

Budgeting for Your Trip

Daily Expenses:

- Accommodation: Budget hotels and hostels can cost between €20-€60 per night, mid-range hotels €60-€150, and luxury hotels €150 and above.
- Food: Budget €5-€15 for a meal at a casual eatery, €15-€40 at mid-range restaurants, and €40 and above for fine dining.
- Transportation: Public transport (buses, trams, metros) costs around €1.50-€3 per trip. Taxis start at €3.50, with

an average fare within city limits being €6-€12. Car rentals start at around €20-€30 per day.

- Attractions: Entry fees for museums and attractions range from €5-€15. Many churches and parks are free or have a nominal fee.

Example Daily Budget:

- Budget Traveler: €50-€80 (Hostel stay, meals at local cafes, public transport)
- Mid-Range Traveler: €100-€200 (3-star hotel, meals at mid-range restaurants, some taxi rides, and paid attractions)
- Luxury Traveler: €200 and above (4-5 star hotels, fine dining, car rental, and premium attractions)

Managing Money

Payment Methods:

- Credit and Debit Cards: Widely accepted, especially Visa and MasterCard. American Express is less commonly accepted.

- Cash: Useful for small purchases, local markets, and rural areas where card payments may not be available.
- ATMs: Widely available and usually offer the best exchange rates. Withdraw larger amounts to minimize fees.

Tipping:

- Tipping is not mandatory but appreciated. A 5-10% tip in restaurants is customary if service is good.
- Round up taxi fares to the nearest euro.
- Tip hotel porters €1-€2 per bag and housekeeping €1-€2 per day.

Cost-Saving Tips
- Travel Off-Season: Visit during spring or autumn for lower accommodation and flight prices.

- Public Transport: Use public transportation instead of taxis. Purchase day passes or multi-day travel cards for savings.

- Eat Like a Local: Dine at local tavernas and markets instead of touristy restaurants. Try the "prato do dia" (dish of the day) for good value.

- Free Attractions: Take advantage of free or low-cost attractions, such as parks, beaches, and certain museums on free admission days.

- Accommodation: Consider staying in budget hotels, hostels, or guesthouses. Airbnb and similar platforms can offer good deals, especially for longer stays.

Financial Safety

- Secure Your Belongings: Keep cash, cards, and important documents in a secure place. Use hotel safes when available.
- Notify Your Bank: Inform your bank of your travel dates to avoid having your cards blocked for suspicious activity.
- Emergency Funds: Carry a backup credit card and some emergency cash in case of lost or stolen cards.

By planning your budget and understanding money matters in Portugal, you can ensure a stress-free and enjoyable trip, making the most of your time in this beautiful and culturally rich country.

Travel Insurance and Health Tips for Your Trip to Portugal

Travel Insurance

Travel insurance is an essential part of planning your trip to Portugal. It provides financial protection and peace of mind in case of unexpected events. Here's what you need to know about securing the right travel insurance and staying healthy during your visit.

Why You Need Travel Insurance:

- Medical Emergencies: Covers the cost of medical treatment, hospital stays, and emergency evacuation.
- Trip Cancellations: Reimburses non-refundable expenses if you need to cancel or interrupt your trip due to covered reasons such as illness, injury, or unforeseen events.
- Lost or Stolen Belongings: Provides compensation for lost, stolen, or damaged luggage and personal items.
- Travel Delays: Covers additional expenses incurred due to flight delays or cancellations.

Types of Coverage:

- Medical Insurance: Essential for covering unexpected health issues. Look for policies with at least €30,000 in medical coverage, as required by the Schengen visa regulations.
- Trip Cancellation and Interruption: Protects your financial investment in case your trip is disrupted.
- Baggage and Personal Belongings: Covers loss or damage to your belongings.
- Emergency Evacuation and Repatriation: Ensures you can be transported to a medical facility or back home in case of a serious medical issue.

How to Choose a Policy:

- Compare Plans: Evaluate different insurance providers and plans based on coverage limits, exclusions, and premiums.
- Read the Fine Print: Understand what is covered and any exclusions that may apply. Common exclusions include pre-existing medical conditions and high-risk activities.

- Check Reviews: Look for customer reviews and ratings to gauge the reliability and service quality of the insurance provider.

Health Tips

Before You Travel:

- Vaccinations: Ensure you are up-to-date on routine vaccinations (measles, mumps, rubella, diphtheria, tetanus, pertussis, varicella, polio, and your annual flu shot). No specific vaccinations are required for Portugal but check for any updates before you travel.
- Health Check-up: Visit your doctor for a pre-travel health check-up, especially if you have chronic conditions.
- Medications: Carry an adequate supply of any prescription medications you take, along with copies of your prescriptions.

During Your Trip:

- Stay Hydrated: Drink plenty of water, especially during the warmer months.

- Sun Protection: Use sunscreen, wear hats, and stay in the shade during peak sun hours to avoid sunburn.

- Food and Water Safety: Tap water is generally safe to drink in Portugal. Enjoy local cuisine, but be cautious with street food and ensure it's prepared and served hygienically.

- Rest and Relax: Travel can be exhausting. Ensure you get enough rest and avoid over-scheduling your days.

Emergency Contacts and Services:

- Emergency Number: Dial 112 for medical emergencies, fire, or police assistance.

- Pharmacies: Look for pharmacies (farmácias) marked with a green cross. Pharmacists can provide advice and medication for minor ailments.

- Hospitals and Clinics: Familiarize yourself with the location of nearby hospitals or medical clinics, especially if you have specific health needs.

COVID-19 Considerations:

- Check Entry Requirements: Stay updated on Portugal's entry requirements related to COVID-19, including testing, vaccination, and quarantine rules.

- Health and Safety Protocols: Follow local guidelines regarding mask-wearing, social distancing, and hygiene practices.

- Travel Insurance: Ensure your travel insurance covers COVID-19-related medical expenses and trip disruptions.

Health and Safety Tips:

- Avoid Bug Bites: While Portugal has a low risk of insect-borne diseases, use insect repellent if you're spending time in nature.

- Stay Active: Portugal offers numerous opportunities for outdoor activities. Engage in walking tours, hikes, and water sports to stay active.
- Emergency Contact Information: Carry a list of emergency contacts, including local medical facilities, your insurance provider's hotline, and the nearest embassy or consulate.

By securing comprehensive travel insurance and following these health tips, you can ensure a safe and enjoyable trip to Portugal, ready to explore all the beauty and culture it has to offer.

Chapter 3

Getting to Know Portugal

Nestled on the western edge of Europe, Portugal is a country rich in history, culture, and natural beauty. Bordered by Spain to the east and the Atlantic Ocean to the west, Portugal offers a unique blend of old-world charm and modern vibrancy. This chapter will introduce you to the essential aspects of Portugal, from its historical roots to its contemporary culture, providing a solid foundation for your travels.

Historical Highlights

Portugal's history is a tapestry woven with diverse influences and significant events. Here's a brief look at the key historical periods that have shaped the nation:

- Prehistoric and Roman Era: Portugal's earliest inhabitants date back to prehistoric times, with significant Roman influence beginning in the 2nd century BCE. Roman ruins, such as those in Conímbriga, provide a glimpse into this ancient past.

- Moorish Influence: From the 8th to the 12th centuries, the Moors from North Africa ruled much of the Iberian Peninsula, including Portugal. Their legacy is evident in their architecture, language, and cuisine.

- The Age of Discovery: The 15th and 16th centuries marked Portugal's golden age. Explorers like Vasco da Gama and Ferdinand Magellan expanded Portuguese influence across the globe, establishing a vast maritime empire.

- Restoration and Modern Era: After a period of Spanish rule, Portugal regained its independence in 1640. The 20th century saw significant political changes, including the Carnation Revolution in 1974, which transitioned the country to democracy.

Cultural Insights

Portuguese culture is a vibrant blend of traditions and modernity, deeply rooted in its history and geography. Key elements of Portuguese culture include:

- Language: Portuguese is the official language and is spoken by the entire population. It's a Romance language, sharing similarities with Spanish, but distinct in pronunciation and vocabulary.

- Religion: Roman Catholicism plays a significant role in Portuguese life, with numerous festivals and traditions linked to the church. Important religious sites include the Sanctuary of Fátima, a major pilgrimage destination.
- Music and Dance: Fado, the soulful music of Portugal, is renowned for its expressive and melancholic tunes.

Traditional dances like the Vira and Corridinho are celebrated during festivals and regional fairs.

- Cuisine: Portuguese cuisine is diverse and flavorful, with a focus on fresh ingredients. Staples include seafood, rice, and bread. Popular dishes are bacalhau (salted cod), caldo verde (kale soup), and pastel de nata (custard tart).

Natural Beauty and Landscapes

Portugal's diverse landscapes offer something for every nature lover. The country's geography ranges from mountainous regions to rolling plains and stunning coastlines.

- Northern Portugal: Known for its lush greenery and vineyards, the north is home to the Douro Valley, famous for its wine production, particularly port wine. The Minho region is known for its historical cities like Braga and Guimarães.

- Central Portugal: This region features the Serra da Estrela mountains, the highest range in mainland Portugal, offering hiking and winter sports. The historic city of Coimbra, with its renowned university, is also located here.

- Lisbon and Surroundings: The capital city of Lisbon is a vibrant mix of old and new, with historical neighborhoods like Alfama and modern areas like Parque das Nações. Nearby, Sintra's palaces and Cascais' beaches are popular day-trip destinations.

- Alentejo: Characterized by rolling plains, cork oak forests, and picturesque towns like Évora, Alentejo is known for its tranquil beauty and agricultural produce, including wine and olive oil.

- Algarve: Portugal's southernmost region, the Algarve, is famous for its stunning beaches, cliffs, and golf courses. Coastal towns like Lagos, Albufeira, and Faro attract tourists year-round.

- Madeira and Azores: These Atlantic archipelagos offer unique landscapes, from Madeira's lush Laurisilva forest to the volcanic scenery of the Azores. Both are ideal for hiking, whale watching, and experiencing local culture.

Practical Information

- Getting Around: Portugal boasts a well-developed transport network. Trains and buses connect major cities, while car rentals offer flexibility for exploring rural areas. In cities, trams, metros, and taxis are convenient.

- Accommodation: From luxury hotels to budget hostels, Portugal offers a range of accommodation options.

Consider staying in a pousada (historical inn) for a unique experience.

- Health and Safety: Portugal is generally safe for travelers. Tap water is safe to drink, and public health facilities are of a high standard. Travel insurance is recommended to cover any unexpected medical expenses.

Festivals and Events

Portugal's calendar is filled with vibrant festivals and events that reflect its rich cultural heritage. Some notable celebrations include:

- Carnival (February/March): Celebrated with parades and parties across the country, the most famous being in Madeira and the town of Torres Vedras.

- Santo António Festival (June): Lisbon celebrates its patron saint with street parties, music, and traditional grilled sardines.

- São João Festival (June): Porto's biggest festival, featuring fireworks, music, and street entertainment.

- Festas de São Mateus (August/September): In Viseu, this fair includes concerts, bullfights, and traditional crafts.

Understanding Portugal's historical context, cultural richness, and natural beauty will enhance your travel experience. Whether you're exploring ancient ruins, enjoying a fado performance, savoring local cuisine, or marveling at the scenic landscapes, Portugal's charm is bound to captivate you. This chapter serves as your introduction to the essentials, setting the stage for a deeper dive into the specifics of planning your journey, exploring regions, and discovering hidden gems in the chapters to come.

Regions and Cities Overview

Portugal is a country of captivating contrasts, from bustling cities and historic towns to scenic landscapes and serene beaches. Each region has its own unique charm and character. In this chapter, we'll provide an overview of Portugal's main regions and cities, highlighting what makes each area special and worth visiting.

Northern Portugal

Porto and the Douro Valley

- Porto: Known for its stately bridges, port wine cellars, and historic Ribeira district, Porto is a vibrant city with a rich maritime heritage. Must-see sights include the Livraria Lello, one of the most beautiful bookstores in the world, and the Palácio da Bolsa.

- Douro Valley: Famous for its terraced vineyards and wine production, this UNESCO World Heritage site offers breathtaking scenery and wine-tasting experiences in quintas (wine estates).

Braga and Guimarães

- Braga: Often referred to as the "Portuguese Rome" for its numerous churches, Braga is one of the country's oldest cities. Highlights include the Bom Jesus do Monte sanctuary and the medieval Sé Cathedral.
- Guimarães: Known as the "birthplace of Portugal," Guimarães boasts a well-preserved medieval town center and the imposing Guimarães Castle.

Central Portugal

Coimbra and Aveiro

- Coimbra: Home to one of Europe's oldest universities, Coimbra is a city of academic tradition and historical significance. Visit the Joanina Library and the Monastery of Santa Clara-a-Velha.
- Aveiro: Often called the "Venice of Portugal" for its picturesque canals and colorful boats, Aveiro is also known for its Art Nouveau architecture and sweet treats called ovos moles.

Serra da Estrela and Fátima

- Serra da Estrela: Portugal's highest mountain range offers excellent hiking, skiing, and the famous Serra da Estrela cheese.

- Fátima: A major pilgrimage site, Fátima attracts millions of visitors each year to its Sanctuary of Our Lady of Fátima.

Lisbon Region

Lisbon and Sintra

- Lisbon: Portugal's capital is a city of seven hills, each offering stunning viewpoints over its historic neighborhoods. Key attractions include the Belém Tower, Jerónimos Monastery, and the bustling Praça do Comércio.
- Sintra: A fairy-tale town nestled in the hills, Sintra is renowned for its palaces and gardens. Don't miss the colorful Pena Palace, the Moorish Castle, and the romantic Quinta da Regaleira.

Cascais and Estoril

- Cascais: A charming coastal town known for its sandy beaches, marina, and the scenic Boca do Inferno cliffs.
- Estoril: Famous for its casino, the largest in Europe, and its glamorous past as a haven for exiled royalty and spies during World War II.

Alentejo

Évora and Monsaraz

- Évora: A UNESCO World Heritage site, Évora boasts well-preserved Roman ruins, a Gothic cathedral, and the eerie Chapel of Bones.
- Monsaraz: A medieval village offering stunning views of the Alqueva reservoir and a glimpse into traditional Alentejo life.

Beja and Marvão

- Beja: Known for its historical architecture, Beja features a castle with panoramic views and the Convent of Nossa Senhora da Conceição.
- Marvão: A fortified village perched atop a granite peak, Marvão offers breathtaking vistas and well-preserved medieval structures.

Algarve

Faro and Lagos

- Faro: The gateway to the Algarve, Faro is known for its well-preserved old town, the Arco da Vila, and the stunning Ria Formosa lagoon.
- Lagos: Famous for its dramatic cliffs, golden beaches, and vibrant nightlife. Key attractions include the Ponta da Piedade and the historic city center.

Albufeira and Tavira

- Albufeira: A lively resort town with beautiful beaches, a bustling marina, and a vibrant nightlife scene.
- Tavira: A picturesque town known for its charming architecture, Roman bridge, and serene island beaches.

Madeira and Azores

Madeira

- Funchal: The capital of Madeira, Funchal is known for its botanical gardens, cable car rides, and the vibrant Mercado dos Lavradores.
- Porto Moniz: Famous for its natural volcanic swimming pools and stunning coastal scenery.

Azores

- São Miguel: The largest island in the Azores, São Miguel is known for its volcanic landscapes, hot springs, and the beautiful Sete Cidades crater lakes.
- Pico: Home to Portugal's highest peak, Mount Pico, this island is famous for its vineyards, whale watching, and rugged beauty.

Portugal's diverse regions and cities offer a wealth of experiences, from the historic charm of Porto and Lisbon to the natural beauty of the Douro Valley and the Algarve's stunning beaches. Each area has its own unique appeal, making Portugal a rich tapestry of sights, sounds, and flavors waiting to be explored. In the following chapters, we'll delve deeper into specific destinations, providing detailed guides to help you plan your visit to each captivating region and city.

Lisbon: Portugal's Vibrant Capital

Welcome to Lisbon, the sun-drenched capital of Portugal, where history and modernity intertwine to create a city of endless charm and excitement. Perched on the edge of the Atlantic Ocean, Lisbon is a city that dances to its own rhythm, inviting visitors to explore its scenic hills, vibrant neighborhoods, and rich cultural heritage.

A City of Seven Hills

Lisbon's unique topography is defined by its seven hills, each offering breathtaking views over the city's terracotta rooftops, winding streets, and the sparkling Tagus River. The best way to get to know Lisbon is on foot or by taking one of its iconic yellow trams, which clatter up and down the steep, narrow streets, offering a nostalgic glimpse into the city's past.

Historic Neighborhoods

Start your journey in the historic district of Alfama, the oldest part of the city. This maze of narrow alleys, steep staircases, and hidden courtyards is a place where time seems to stand still. Here, you'll find the majestic São Jorge Castle, which offers panoramic views over Lisbon, and the Lisbon Cathedral, a stunning Romanesque structure dating back to the 12th century.

Head to Baixa, the heart of downtown Lisbon, known for its grand squares, elegant boulevards, and vibrant shopping streets. Don't miss a visit to the Praça do Comércio, a vast waterfront square surrounded by yellow Pombaline buildings, and the Rossio Square, with its distinctive wave-patterned cobblestones.

Avenida da Liberdade and Chiado

For a taste of Lisbon's more sophisticated side, stroll along Avenida da Liberdade, a tree-lined boulevard filled with high-end shops, theaters, and cafés. Nearby, the Chiado district beckons with its blend of old-world charm and contemporary flair. This cultural hub is home to historic cafés, trendy boutiques, and the famous Livraria Bertrand, the world's oldest operating bookstore.

Belém: A Journey Through History

No visit to Lisbon is complete without a trip to Belém, a neighborhood that celebrates Portugal's Age of Discovery. Here, you'll find the iconic Belém Tower and the Jerónimos Monastery, both UNESCO World Heritage sites that showcase the intricate Manueline architecture. Indulge in a pastéis de nata at the renowned Pastéis de Belém, where this delicious custard tart was first created.

Lisbon's Cultural Scene

Lisbon is a city that thrives on creativity and culture. The Calouste Gulbenkian Museum boasts an impressive collection of art, from ancient to modern, while the MAAT

(Museum of Art, Architecture, and Technology) offers a cutting-edge experience in a striking riverside building. Don't miss the vibrant street art that adorns the city's walls, transforming Lisbon into an open-air gallery.

Dining and Nightlife

Lisbon's culinary scene is a feast for the senses, offering everything from traditional Portuguese fare to innovative fusion cuisine. Savor fresh seafood at a seaside restaurant, enjoy a hearty bacalhau dish, or try petiscos, the Portuguese version of tapas, in a cozy taverna. As night falls, the Bairro Alto district comes alive with its lively bars, music venues, and Fado houses, where you can experience the soul-stirring sounds of Portugal's traditional music.

Hidden Gems

Beyond the well-trodden paths, Lisbon is filled with hidden gems waiting to be discovered. Explore the LX Factory, a creative hub housed in a former industrial complex, offering quirky shops, art studios, and trendy eateries. Wander through the enchanting gardens of Estufa Fria, a greenhouse filled with exotic plants, or relax in the tranquil Jardim da Estrela.

A City of Warmth and Welcome

What truly sets Lisbon apart is its warm and welcoming atmosphere. The city's residents, known as Lisboetas, are known for their friendliness and hospitality, always ready to share a story, offer directions, or recommend a favorite local spot.

Lisbon is a city that captures the heart and imagination, offering a perfect blend of history, culture, and contemporary living. Whether you're exploring its ancient landmarks, indulging in its culinary delights, or simply soaking up the sun along its scenic waterfront, Lisbon promises a memorable experience that will leave you longing to return. Welcome to Lisbon – Portugal's vibrant capital, where every corner holds a new adventure.

Porto: City of Bridges and Port Wine

Welcome to Porto, a city that seamlessly blends historic charm with a vibrant contemporary culture. Perched on the hills overlooking the Douro River, Porto is famed for its stunning bridges, world-renowned Port wine, and rich architectural heritage. Known as the "Cidade Invicta" (Unvanquished City), Porto invites you to explore its scenic beauty, savor its culinary delights, and immerse yourself in its lively atmosphere.

The Majestic Bridges

Porto is famously known as the City of Bridges, and for good reason. The most iconic of these is the Dom Luís I Bridge, an iron masterpiece designed by a student of Gustave Eiffel. This double-deck bridge offers panoramic views of the river and connects the bustling Ribeira district with the wine cellars of Vila Nova de Gaia. Another notable bridge is the Arrábida Bridge, with its impressive concrete arch, and the modern Infante Dom Henrique Bridge, showcasing contemporary engineering.

Historic Ribeira

Begin your journey in the Ribeira district, a UNESCO World Heritage site characterized by its narrow, winding streets, colorful buildings, and lively atmosphere. The Ribeira Square, lined with charming cafés and restaurants, is the perfect spot to soak up the vibrant ambiance and enjoy a glass of local wine. Wander along the Cais da Ribeira, the picturesque riverfront promenade, where you can take a leisurely boat cruise to see the city's skyline from the water.

Port Wine Cellars

Porto's fame is inextricably linked to its production of Port wine, a rich and fortified wine that has been crafted in the region for centuries. Cross the Dom Luís I Bridge to Vila Nova de Gaia, where you'll find the historic Port wine cellars. Join a guided tour to learn about the intricate process of making Port wine, and indulge in tastings of various vintages. Renowned names like Sandeman, Taylor's, and Graham's offer exceptional experiences that are both educational and delicious.

Architectural Marvels

Porto is a city of architectural wonders, blending Gothic, Baroque, and modern styles. The Sé do Porto (Porto Cathedral) stands as a testament to the city's medieval heritage, offering stunning views from its terrace. The São Bento Railway Station is another architectural gem, adorned with magnificent azulejos (blue and white tiles) that depict significant moments in Portuguese history.

One of Porto's most iconic landmarks is the Livraria Lello, often cited as one of the most beautiful bookstores in the world. Its neo-Gothic façade, intricate wooden interiors, and majestic staircase make it a must-visit for book lovers and history enthusiasts alike.

A Taste of Porto

Porto's culinary scene is a delightful mix of traditional flavors and contemporary innovation. Savor the city's most famous dish, the Francesinha, a hearty sandwich layered with various meats, smothered in melted cheese, and bathed in a rich beer sauce. Seafood lovers will relish the freshness of local catches, from grilled sardines to octopus salad.

For a sweet treat, don't miss the pastéis de nata (custard tarts) and the region's unique take on desserts, often infused with Port wine. Pair your meals with Vinho Verde, a refreshing and slightly effervescent wine from the nearby Minho region, or enjoy a glass of robust Douro red wine.

Vibrant Culture

Porto is a city pulsating with cultural energy. The Casa da Música, a striking modern concert hall designed by Rem Koolhaas, hosts a diverse range of performances, from classical concerts to contemporary music events. Art enthusiasts will appreciate the Serralves Museum, which features contemporary art exhibitions set within a beautiful park.

The city's traditional festivals, such as São João, bring the streets to life with music, dancing, and fireworks. Join the locals in celebrating with grilled sardines, lively folk music, and the unique tradition of tapping others on the head with plastic hammers.

Hidden Gems

Beyond the main attractions, Porto is brimming with hidden gems waiting to be discovered. Explore the Jardim do Morro, a serene park that offers spectacular views of the city and the Douro River, especially at sunset. Visit the Palácio de Cristal Gardens, a lush oasis with scenic walking paths, peacocks, and panoramic vistas.

The Foz do Douro district, where the river meets the Atlantic Ocean, is perfect for a leisurely stroll along the seaside promenade, dotted with charming cafés and historic fortresses. For a unique experience, visit the São Francisco Church, known for its lavish Baroque interior covered in gold leaf.

A Warm Welcome

What truly sets Porto apart is its warm and welcoming spirit. The tripeiros, as the residents of Porto are affectionately known, are known for their hospitality and pride in their city's heritage. Whether you're navigating the bustling markets, enjoying a riverside meal, or exploring historic sites, you'll be met with friendly faces and genuine warmth.

Porto is a city that captivates the senses and the soul, offering a rich tapestry of history, culture, and natural beauty. Whether you're wandering its historic streets, savoring its culinary delights, or simply enjoying the breathtaking views, Porto promises an unforgettable experience that will leave you enchanted. Welcome to Porto – the City of Bridges and Port Wine, where every moment is a journey of discovery.

The Algarve: Stunning Coastline and Beaches

Welcome to the Algarve, Portugal's sun-drenched southern region, renowned for its breathtaking coastline, golden beaches, and charming villages. Whether you're seeking thrilling water sports, tranquil beach days, or picturesque landscapes, the Algarve offers something for everyone. Let's explore what makes this region a must-visit destination.

The Allure of the Algarve

The Algarve stretches from the Spanish border to the rugged cliffs of the southwestern tip of Europe. With over 200 kilometers of coastline, this region is home to some of the most stunning beaches in the world. Crystal-clear waters, dramatic cliffs, hidden coves, and expansive sandy shores make the Algarve a beach lover's paradise.

Top Beaches to Visit

Praia da Marinha

Often ranked among the best beaches in the world, Praia da Marinha is a true gem. Its iconic limestone cliffs, crystal-clear waters, and sea arches create a picturesque setting perfect for swimming, snorkeling, or simply relaxing under the sun.

Benagil Cave

One of the Algarve's most famous landmarks, the Benagil Cave, is a must-see. Accessible only by boat, kayak, or paddleboard, this sea cave with its stunning skylight offers a magical experience. Nearby Benagil Beach serves as the starting point for many of these adventures.

Praia da Falésia

Stretching for nearly 6 kilometers, Praia da Falésia is known for its striking red and white cliffs. The long sandy beach is perfect for long walks, sunbathing, and water sports. The cliffs also provide a beautiful backdrop for photos.

Praia do Camilo

Nestled between Lagos and the Ponta da Piedade headland, Praia do Camilo is a small but stunning beach. A wooden staircase descends to the golden sands, where you can explore rock formations, clear waters, and marine life.

Coastal Villages and Towns

Lagos

Lagos combines historical charm with vibrant nightlife and stunning beaches. Visit the historic old town with its cobbled streets, explore the 17th-century fort, and relax on the nearby beaches like Praia Dona Ana and Meia Praia.

Albufeira

Once a small fishing village, Albufeira is now a bustling tourist hotspot. Its lively nightlife, family-friendly activities, and beautiful beaches like Praia dos Pescadores and Praia da Oura make it a popular destination.

Tavira

Tavira offers a more tranquil experience with its charming architecture, Roman bridge, and serene beaches. Take a short ferry ride to the Ilha de Tavira for pristine sandy shores and clear waters.

Water Sports and Activities

The Algarve's coastline isn't just for relaxing; it's also a playground for adventure seekers.

Surfing

The region's western coast, particularly around Sagres, is known for its excellent surf spots. Whether you're a beginner or an experienced surfer, the consistent waves provide great conditions.

Kayaking and Paddleboarding

Explore the Algarve's stunning sea caves and hidden coves by kayak or paddleboard. Guided tours often depart from

Lagos, Albufeira, and Benagil, providing safe and exciting ways to discover the coastline.

Dolphin Watching

The waters off the Algarve are home to various marine life, including dolphins. Boat tours from Lagos, Albufeira, and Portimão offer the chance to see these playful creatures in their natural habitat.

Natural Parks and Scenic Routes

Ria Formosa Natural Park

A haven for birdwatchers and nature enthusiasts, Ria Formosa is a protected area of lagoons, marshes, and islands. Explore the park by boat or on foot to discover its diverse wildlife and scenic beauty.

Costa Vicentina

The Costa Vicentina is part of the Southwest Alentejo and Vicentine Coast Natural Park. This rugged stretch of coastline offers stunning views, hiking trails, and secluded beaches, perfect for those seeking solitude and natural beauty.

Culinary Delights

The Algarve's cuisine is as rich and diverse as its landscapes. Fresh seafood is a staple, with dishes like cataplana (seafood stew), grilled sardines, and octopus salad being local favorites. Don't miss out on the region's sweet treats, such as pastéis de nata and the fig and almond desserts.

Festivals and Events

The Algarve hosts various festivals and events throughout the year, celebrating everything from seafood to music.

Festival do Marisco

Held in Olhão, the Seafood Festival showcases the region's best seafood with live music and entertainment.

Carvoeiro Black & White Night

This summer festival in Carvoeiro features live music, DJs, and a dress code of black and white, transforming the town into a vibrant party scene.

Practical Tips for Visiting the Algarve

- **Best Time to Visit**: The Algarve is a year-round destination, but the best time to visit is from late spring to early autumn when the weather is warm and the sea is inviting.
- **Getting Around:** Renting a car is the best way to explore the Algarve, giving you the flexibility to visit remote beaches and villages at your own pace.

- **Accommodation**: From luxury resorts to charming guesthouses, the Algarve offers a range of accommodation options to suit every budget.

The Algarve's stunning coastline, beautiful beaches, and vibrant towns make it a top destination in Portugal. Whether you're seeking relaxation, adventure, or cultural experiences, this region offers it all. Dive into the crystal-clear waters, explore hidden coves, and enjoy the rich flavors of the local cuisine – the Algarve awaits your discovery.

Coimbra: Historical University Town

Welcome to Coimbra, a city that beautifully blends rich history with vibrant student life. Nestled along the banks of the Mondego River, Coimbra is renowned for its prestigious university, captivating medieval architecture, and lively cultural scene. Let's explore what makes this historical university town a must-visit destination in Portugal.

The Heart of Coimbra: University of Coimbra

A Storied Past

The University of Coimbra, founded in 1290, is one of the oldest universities in the world and the oldest in Portugal. Its historical significance and academic prestige have earned it a UNESCO World Heritage designation. The university's sprawling campus is a treasure trove of architectural marvels and historical artifacts.

Joanina Library

The Joanina Library, an 18th-century Baroque masterpiece, is a highlight of the university. Housing over 200,000 volumes, the library's ornate interiors, with gilded woodwork and frescoed ceilings, offer a glimpse into the grandeur of Coimbra's academic heritage. It's not just a place for books but a symbol of the intellectual spirit that has thrived in Coimbra for centuries.

University Tower

The University Tower, or "Torre da Universidade," offers panoramic views of the city and the river. Climbing its steps is a rite of passage for many students and visitors, rewarding them with breathtaking vistas and a sense of the university's prominent place in the cityscape.

Wandering Through Coimbra's Old Town

Sé Velha (Old Cathedral)

Coimbra's Old Cathedral, Sé Velha, is a Romanesque gem dating back to the 12th century. Its fortress-like appearance, with crenelated walls and a massive façade, speaks to its historical role as a place of worship and defense. Inside, the cathedral's cloisters and Gothic chapels offer a serene escape into history.

Santa Cruz Monastery

Founded in 1131, the Santa Cruz Monastery is a key landmark in Coimbra. It is the final resting place of Portugal's first kings, Afonso Henriques and Sancho I. The monastery's intricate Manueline architecture and serene cloisters make it a peaceful place to reflect on Portugal's royal past.

Almedina Arch

The Almedina Arch, a remnant of Coimbra's medieval walls, is an iconic entry point to the old town. Passing through this ancient gateway, you'll find yourself in a labyrinth of narrow streets, filled with cafes, shops, and traditional houses, each corner echoing with centuries of history.

Student Life and Traditions

Fado de Coimbra

Coimbra is famous for its unique style of Fado, a melancholic genre of music traditionally performed by university students. Fado de Coimbra is distinguished by its themes of love, longing, and academic life. Attending a live Fado performance in one of Coimbra's traditional venues is an unforgettable experience that captures the soul of the city.

Academic Rituals

Coimbra's academic traditions are colorful and enduring. The "Queima das Fitas" (Burning of the Ribbons) is a week-long celebration marking the end of the academic year, filled with parades, concerts, and festivities. Students, dressed in their traditional black capes, burn their ribbons in a symbolic gesture of transition.

Exploring the Natural Beauty

Mondego River

The serene Mondego River flows through Coimbra, offering picturesque views and leisurely activities. Stroll along the riverbanks, enjoy a picnic in the Parque Verde do Mondego, or take a boat ride to see the city from a different perspective.

Botanical Garden

The Botanical Garden of the University of Coimbra, established in the 18th century, is a lush retreat within the city. Covering 13 hectares, the garden features exotic plants, serene ponds, and shaded pathways. It's a perfect spot for a relaxing walk and a deeper appreciation of nature.

Culinary Delights

Traditional Cuisine

Coimbra's culinary scene is rich with traditional Portuguese flavors. Savor "Leitão à Bairrada" (roast suckling pig) or "Chanfana" (goat stew), both regional specialties. For dessert, try "Pastéis de Santa Clara," a sweet pastry filled with almond and egg yolk, named after the nearby Convent of Santa Clara.

Bustling Markets and Cozy Cafés

Mercado D. Pedro V is a bustling market where you can find fresh produce, local cheeses, and traditional pastries. The city's cafés, especially those near the university, are perfect for enjoying a coffee and a pastel de nata while soaking in the vibrant atmosphere.

Coimbra is more than just a university town; it's a living museum, a hub of academic excellence, and a vibrant community where history and modernity coexist harmoniously. From its storied university and medieval landmarks to its lively student traditions and picturesque natural settings, Coimbra offers a rich tapestry of experiences. Whether you're a history buff, a cultural enthusiast, or simply a curious traveler, Coimbra invites you to discover its many charms and be part of its enduring legacy.

Sintra: Fairytale Palaces and Gardens

Nestled in the foothills of the Sintra Mountains, just a short drive from Lisbon lies the enchanting town of Sintra. Known for its lush landscapes, mystical forests, and a collection of palaces and castles that look straight out of a storybook, Sintra is a must-visit destination for anyone traveling to Portugal. In this chapter, we will explore the magical allure of Sintra, highlighting its key attractions, historic significance, and the best ways to experience its fairytale charm.

Key Attractions

Pena Palace (Palácio da Pena)

- Overview: One of the most iconic landmarks in Portugal, Pena Palace sits atop a hill and offers panoramic views of the surrounding landscape. The palace is a masterpiece of 19th-century Romanticism, blending Gothic, Manueline, Moorish, and Renaissance architectural styles.

- Highlights: Explore the vibrant exterior with its striking colors and intricate details. Inside, the palace is richly decorated with period furnishings and artifacts. Don't miss the surrounding park, which features winding paths, exotic plants, and hidden lakes.

Quinta da Regaleira

- Overview: A UNESCO World Heritage site, Quinta da Regaleira is an enigmatic estate with a palace, chapel, and expansive gardens. Designed by Italian architect Luigi Manini, the estate is known for its Gothic, Renaissance, and Manueline architecture, as well as its mystical symbolism.
- Highlights: The Initiation Well is a must-see, with its spiral staircase leading down into the earth, symbolizing a journey to the center of the world. The gardens are filled with

grottoes, fountains, and secret tunnels that invite exploration and discovery.

Moorish Castle (Castelo dos Mouros)

- Overview: This medieval castle dates back to the 8th and 9th centuries when the Moors controlled the Iberian Peninsula. Perched on a high cliff, the castle offers stunning views over Sintra and the Atlantic coast.
- Highlights: Walk along the ancient ramparts, explore the towers, and enjoy the breathtaking vistas. The castle's history is brought to life through informative displays and well-preserved ruins.

Sintra National Palace (Palácio Nacional de Sintra)

- Overview: Located in the heart of Sintra, this palace was a royal residence from the early 15th to the late 19th century.

It is notable for its mix of Gothic, Manueline, and Mudéjar styles, as well as its distinctive twin chimneys.

- Highlights: Inside, you'll find elaborately decorated rooms, such as the Swan Room, the Magpie Room, and the Arab Room, each with unique tiles and frescoes. The palace also boasts an impressive collection of azulejos (Portuguese tiles).

Monserrate Palace (Palácio de Monserrate)

- Overview: Monserrate Palace is an exotic villa surrounded by lush botanical gardens. Built-in the 19th century, it showcases Romantic, Gothic, and Moorish influences.
- Highlights: The palace's richly decorated interiors and intricate stonework are complemented by the stunning gardens, which feature rare and exotic plants from around

the world. The park is a serene place for a leisurely stroll or a picnic.

Historic Significance

Sintra's significance dates back centuries, serving as a retreat for Portuguese royalty and aristocrats. The town's unique microclimate, with cooler temperatures and lush vegetation, made it an ideal escape from the heat of Lisbon. Over the years, Sintra has attracted artists, writers, and travelers, enchanted by its mystical aura and architectural beauty.

UNESCO World Heritage Site:
- In 1995, the Cultural Landscape of Sintra was designated a UNESCO World Heritage site, recognizing its historical and cultural importance, as well as its unique blend of natural and man-made beauty.

Experiencing Sintra

Getting There:

- From Lisbon: Sintra is easily accessible from Lisbon by train, with regular services departing from Rossio Station. The journey takes approximately 40 minutes. Alternatively, you can drive or take a guided tour.

Exploring the Town:

- On Foot: The town center of Sintra is compact and walkable, with narrow streets, charming shops, and local cafes. It's the perfect place to start your exploration.
- Public Transport: Sintra has a convenient bus system that connects the main attractions. The hop-on-hop-off buses are particularly useful for visitors.
- Tuk-Tuks and Carriages: For a more unique experience, consider taking a tuk-tuk or horse-drawn carriage ride to explore the town and its surroundings.

Best Time to Visit:

- Sintra can be visited year-round, but spring (March to May) and autumn (September to November) offer pleasant weather and fewer crowds. Summer is the peak tourist season, so expect larger crowds and plan accordingly.

Local Delicacies:

- Travesseiros: A delicious puff pastry filled with almond cream, typically enjoyed with a cup of coffee.
- Queijadas de Sintra: Traditional cheese tarts that are sweet and creamy, a perfect treat to savor as you explore the town.

Sintra's enchanting palaces, lush gardens, and rich history make it a true fairytale destination. Whether you're wandering through the colorful halls of Pena Palace, descending into the mystical depths of the Initiation Well, or strolling through the serene gardens of Monserrate, Sintra offers an unforgettable experience. In the next chapters, we will continue to explore the diverse regions of Portugal, each with its own unique attractions and charm, guiding you through the best this beautiful country has to offer.

Douro Valley: Wine Country and River Cruises

The Douro Valley, renowned for its stunning landscapes and rich viticultural heritage, is one of Portugal's most captivating regions. Stretching along the Douro River from the Spanish border to the vibrant city of Porto, this UNESCO World Heritage site offers a blend of scenic beauty, historic vineyards, and charming towns. In this guide, we'll explore the best ways to experience the Douro Valley, from wine tasting at historic quintas to leisurely river cruises.

Scenic Beauty and Historic Vineyards

The Douro Valley's dramatic landscapes are characterized by steep, terraced vineyards that rise majestically from the riverbanks. This region has been producing wine for over 2,000 years, making it one of the oldest wine-producing areas in the world. The vineyards, or quintas, are primarily known for producing port wine, but they also produce excellent red and white table wines.

Highlights:

- Terraced Vineyards: The terraced vineyards are a testament to centuries of agricultural innovation and hard work. They offer a breathtaking sight, particularly in the autumn when the leaves change color.
- Quintas: Visiting a Quinta is a must. These wine estates often include tours of the vineyards, wine cellars, and tastings. Some notable quintas include Quinta do Seixo, Quinta do Crasto, and Quinta da Pacheca.

River Cruises

One of the most relaxing and scenic ways to explore the Douro Valley is by taking a river cruise. Cruises range from short half-day trips to multi-day excursions, allowing visitors to experience the region from the serene vantage point of the Douro River.

Types of Cruises:

- Day Cruises: Short cruises typically depart from Porto or Peso da Régua and provide stunning views of the terraced vineyards and picturesque villages along the riverbanks.
- Multi-Day Cruises: These longer cruises often include stops at various quintas for wine tasting, as well as guided tours of historic towns and landmarks.

Highlights:

- Scenic Views: The river cruises offer unparalleled views of the valley's dramatic landscapes, with opportunities to see traditional rabelo boats, and historic wine transport vessels, gliding along the river.

- Locks and Dams: The Douro River features a series of impressive locks and dams that boats must navigate, providing a unique aspect of the journey.

- Cultural Insights: Many cruises include commentary on the history and culture of the Douro Valley, enriching the experience with local knowledge and stories.

Charming Towns and Villages

The Douro Valley is dotted with charming towns and villages, each with its own unique character and attractions. These towns offer a glimpse into the region's history and culture, with historic architecture, local markets, and traditional festivals.

Highlights:

- Peso da Régua: Often considered the gateway to the Douro Valley, this town is home to the Douro Museum, which provides an excellent overview of the region's wine-making history.

- Pinhão: Nestled in the heart of the valley, Pinhão is surrounded by some of the most famous quintas. The Pinhão Railway Station is renowned for its beautiful azulejo (tile) panels depicting scenes of the Douro Valley.

- Lamego: Known for its baroque architecture, Lamego boasts the stunning Sanctuary of Nossa Senhora dos Remédios, which sits atop a grand staircase of nearly 700 steps.

Wine Tasting and Gastronomy

Wine tasting in the Douro Valley is a sensory delight. Visitors can sample a variety of wines, from the world-famous port to robust reds and crisp whites. The region's gastronomy is equally impressive, featuring hearty, traditional Portuguese dishes that pair perfectly with the local wines.

Highlights:

- Wine Tastings: Most quintas offer guided tastings, where visitors can learn about the wine-making process and the distinct characteristics of Douro wines. Look for tastings that include a variety of wines, including vintage ports and reserve reds.
- Local Cuisine: The Douro Valley's cuisine is rustic and flavorful. Try dishes like cozido à portuguesa (a traditional Portuguese stew), bacalhau (salted cod), and local cheeses. Many quintas have on-site restaurants that offer delicious meals with stunning vineyard views.
- Wine and Food Pairing: Experience the art of pairing Douro wines with local dishes, enhancing the flavors of

both the food and the wine. Some quintas offer specialized wine and food pairing experiences.

Practical Information

Getting There:

- By Car: Driving from Porto to the Douro Valley takes about 1.5 to 2 hours. The scenic routes offer spectacular views and the flexibility to stop at various points of interest.
- By Train: Trains run regularly from Porto to towns like Peso da Régua and Pinhão, providing a scenic and relaxing journey along the Douro River.
- By Boat: River cruises from Porto to the Douro Valley are a popular and picturesque option, though they may take longer than traveling by car or train.

Best Time to Visit:

- Spring (March to May): Offers pleasant weather, blooming flowers, and fewer tourists.

- Autumn (September to November): Harvest season is a particularly beautiful and vibrant time to visit, with the vineyards turning shades of red and gold.

Accommodation:
- The Douro Valley offers a range of accommodation options, from luxurious wine hotels and charming guesthouses to rustic farm stays. Staying at a Quinta can provide an immersive experience in the heart of the vineyards.

The Douro Valley is a region of extraordinary beauty and rich heritage. Whether you're sipping wine at a historic Quinta, cruising along the serene Douro River, or exploring the charming towns and villages, the Douro Valley offers a memorable experience that captures the essence of Portugal's wine country. This picturesque region invites you to slow down, savor its delights, and immerse yourself in its timeless landscapes and traditions.

Chapter 4

Top Attractions and Landmarks

Welcome to the heart of Portugal's allure, where history, culture, and natural beauty converge to create an unforgettable travel experience. This chapter will guide you through the top attractions and landmarks that define this captivating country. From the ancient streets of Lisbon and Porto to the enchanting landscapes of Sintra, the sun-drenched beaches of the Algarve, and the lush, volcanic islands of Madeira and the Azores, Portugal offers a rich tapestry of sights and experiences.

Discovering Portugal's Highlights

In this chapter, we will embark on a journey through Portugal's most iconic destinations, exploring the historical significance, architectural grandeur, and natural wonders that make each site unique. Whether you are a history buff, a nature lover, or simply looking to immerse yourself in the local culture, Portugal's top attractions provide something for everyone.

Lisbon: A Historic Capital

Our exploration begins in Lisbon, Portugal's vibrant capital, where centuries-old monuments stand alongside contemporary cultural hotspots. From the majestic Belém Tower, a symbol of Portugal's Age of Discoveries, to the ornate Jerónimos Monastery and the commanding São Jorge Castle, Lisbon is a city where the past and present coexist harmoniously.

Porto: Charm and Character

Next, we travel to Porto, a city renowned for its picturesque riverside, historic bridges, and world-famous port wine. The Dom Luís I Bridge offers stunning views of the Douro River, while Livraria Lello captivates visitors with its Art Nouveau beauty. Clérigos Tower stands tall as a testament to Porto's rich architectural heritage.

Sintra: A Fairytale Retreat

Nestled in the Sintra Mountains, the town of Sintra is a fairytale come to life. The vibrant Pena Palace, the mysterious Quinta da Regaleira, and the ancient Moorish Castle each tell stories of royal opulence and romantic escapades, set against a backdrop of lush, green hills.

Algarve: Coastal Paradise

For those seeking sun and sea, the Algarve region offers some of Portugal's most stunning coastal scenery. From the dramatic cliffs and sea caves of Ponta da Piedade to the iconic Benagil Cave and the windswept Cape St. Vincent, the Algarve is a paradise for beach lovers and adventurers alike.

Madeira: Island Bliss

The island of Madeira beckons with its unique landscapes and botanical wonders. Explore the ancient Laurisilva Forest, step out onto the glass-floored skywalk at Cabo Girão, and relax in the serene Monte Palace Tropical Garden. Madeira's natural beauty and mild climate make it a year-round destination.

Azores: Nature's Playground

Finally, we venture to the Azores, an archipelago of volcanic islands known for their stunning natural beauty and outdoor adventures. From the twin lakes of Sete Cidades on São Miguel Island to the geothermal wonders of Furnas and the towering Mount Pico on Pico Island, the Azores offer a wealth of experiences for nature enthusiasts.

A Journey Through Time and Beauty

This chapter will provide an in-depth look at each of these top attractions and landmarks, offering insights into their historical significance, unique features, and practical tips for visitors. Whether you are planning your first trip to Portugal or seeking to rediscover its many treasures, join us as we uncover the highlights that make this country a truly remarkable destination.

UNESCO World Heritage Sites in Portugal

Portugal, with its rich history and diverse cultural heritage, is home to numerous UNESCO World Heritage Sites. These sites are recognized for their outstanding universal value and offer a window into the country's past, from ancient monasteries and historic city centers to unique natural landscapes. In this section, we explore some of Portugal's most significant UNESCO World Heritage Sites.

Belém Tower (Torre de Belém)

Location: Lisbon

Overview:

The Belém Tower, a symbol of Portugal's maritime discoveries, stands proudly on the banks of the Tagus River in Lisbon. Built in the early 16th century, this fortress is a remarkable example of Manueline architecture, characterized by intricate stone carvings and maritime motifs.

Highlights:

- Climb to the top for panoramic views of the river and the city.
- Explore the bastions and the watchtowers adorned with ornate battlements.
- Discover the interior chambers, including the king's hall and the dungeon below sea level.

Jerónimos Monastery (Mosteiro dos Jerónimos)

Location: Lisbon

Overview:

Also located in Lisbon's Belém district, the Jerónimos Monastery is a masterpiece of Manueline architecture. Commissioned by King Manuel I to commemorate Vasco da Gama's successful voyage to India, the monastery is a testament to Portugal's Age of Discoveries.

Highlights:

- Admire the elaborate stone carvings depicting nautical themes.
- Visit the tomb of Vasco da Gama and other notable figures.
- Stroll through the serene cloisters and marvel at the detailed arches and columns.

Location: Porto

Overview:

Porto, Portugal's second-largest city, boasts a historic center that is a UNESCO World Heritage Site. The area is known for its narrow medieval streets, colorful houses, and significant landmarks that reflect Porto's rich commercial history.

Highlights:

- Walk across the Dom Luís I Bridge for stunning views of the Douro River.
- Explore the Ribeira district with its lively waterfront and charming cafes.
- Visit the Sé Cathedral and the iconic Clérigos Tower.

Location: Batalha

Overview:

The Monastery of Batalha, a stunning Gothic and Manueline masterpiece, was built to commemorate the Portuguese victory over the Castilians at the Battle of Aljubarrota in 1385. This monumental structure is a symbol of national pride and architectural splendor.

Highlights:

- Explore the church with its impressive stained glass windows and intricate stonework.
- Visit the Founder's Chapel, which houses the tomb of King João I and his wife, Philippa of Lancaster.
- Wander through the cloisters and admire the elaborate detailing.

Convent of Christ in Tomar

Location: Tomar

Overview:

The Convent of Christ in Tomar is a historic and architectural gem, originally a Templar stronghold. The convent complex showcases a blend of Romanesque, Gothic, Manueline, and Renaissance styles, reflecting its long history and significance.

Highlights:

- Discover the Charola, the Templar's oratory with its stunning frescoes and octagonal design.
- Explore the Manueline window, an elaborate masterpiece of sculptural decoration.
- Wander through the various cloisters, each with unique architectural elements.

Douro Valley

Location: Northern Portugal

Overview:

The Douro Valley is renowned for its stunning landscapes and terraced vineyards that produce the world-famous Port wine. This region, recognized for its cultural and natural value, offers breathtaking views and a deep connection to viticultural traditions.

Highlights:

- Visit historic Quintas (wine estates) and sample a variety of local wines.
- Take a river cruise along the Douro River to appreciate the terraced vineyards and scenic beauty.
- Explore the charming towns and villages that dot the valley.

Sintra Cultural Landscape

Location: Sintra

Overview:

The town of Sintra, with its lush landscapes and romantic architecture, has long been a favorite retreat for Portuguese royalty. The Sintra Cultural Landscape encompasses a variety of historic estates, gardens, and palaces, set amidst the Sintra Mountains.

Highlights:

- Visit the whimsical Pena Palace, a colorful blend of architectural styles.
- Explore the mysterious Quinta da Regaleira with its symbolic gardens and initiation well.
- Discover the Moorish Castle, offering panoramic views of the surrounding area.

Location: Coimbra

Overview:

The University of Coimbra, one of the oldest universities in Europe, is a historic and cultural landmark. Its complex includes magnificent buildings that showcase a range of architectural styles, from medieval to baroque.

Highlights:

- Visit the stunning Joanina Library, adorned with rich baroque decorations.
- Explore the Royal Palace of Alcáçova and the university's historic courtyards.
- Discover the Chapel of São Miguel with its beautiful azulejos (tiles) and intricate organ.

Historic Centre of Évora

Location: Évora

Overview:

Évora, a city in the Alentejo region, is known for its well-preserved historic center, which reflects a mix of Roman, Gothic, and Manueline architecture. The city's rich history and cultural heritage are evident in its many landmarks.

Highlights:

- Visit the Roman Temple, also known as the Temple of Diana.
- Explore the Gothic Évora Cathedral with its impressive views from the rooftop.
- Wander through the narrow streets and discover the charming Praça do Giraldo.

Laurisilva of Madeira

Location: Madeira Island

Overview:

The Laurisilva of Madeira is a rare and ancient laurel forest that covers much of the island's mountainous interior. This UNESCO World Heritage site is known for its unique biodiversity and pristine natural beauty.

Highlights:

- Hike through the lush, misty forests filled with endemic plant species.
- Discover waterfalls, streams, and breathtaking vistas along the trails.
- Experience the tranquility and ecological importance of this ancient forest.

Portugal's UNESCO World Heritage Sites offer a rich and diverse tapestry of cultural, historical, and natural wonders. Each site tells a unique story, reflecting the country's long and varied history, architectural achievements, and natural beauty. Whether exploring the historic streets of Porto, marveling at the Manueline splendor of Lisbon's monuments, or wandering through the ancient forests of Madeira, these sites provide a deep and enriching experience for travelers.

Castles, Palaces, and Fortresses in Portugal

Portugal is a land of enchantment, where medieval castles, opulent palaces, and formidable fortresses dot the landscape, each bearing witness to the country's rich and tumultuous history. These architectural marvels not only showcase Portugal's artistic and military prowess but also offer a glimpse into the lives of the royalty, nobility, and soldiers who once inhabited them. In this section, we explore some of Portugal's most iconic castles, palaces, and fortresses.

Castles

São Jorge Castle (Castelo de São Jorge)

Location: Lisbon

Overview:

São Jorge Castle stands atop one of Lisbon's highest hills, offering panoramic views of the city and the Tagus River. Originally built by the Moors in the mid-11th century, this castle has played a crucial role in the city's history, serving as a royal palace, military stronghold, and now, a popular tourist attraction.

Highlights:

- Explore the castle's ancient walls and towers.
- Visit the archaeological site within the castle grounds, which includes remnants from the Iron Age.
- Enjoy stunning views of Lisbon from the castle's vantage points.

Castle of the Moors (Castelo dos Mouros)

Location: Sintra

Overview:

Nestled in the Sintra Mountains, the Castle of the Moors is a medieval fortress that dates back to the 8th and 9th centuries, built by the Moors to protect the region. The castle offers a rugged charm with its stone walls and breathtaking views over Sintra and the Atlantic Ocean.

Highlights:

- Walk along the ramparts and take in the panoramic views.
- Explore the ancient walls, towers, and cistern.
- Discover the castle's rich history and its strategic importance during the Reconquista.

Guimarães Castle (Castelo de Guimarães)

Location: Guimarães

Overview:

Known as the "birthplace of Portugal," Guimarães Castle is a symbol of the nation's founding. Constructed in the 10th century, this castle played a pivotal role in the formation of Portugal and is closely associated with the first King of Portugal, Afonso I.

Highlights:

- Climb the keep for panoramic views of the city.
- Explore the castle's walls and towers.
- Learn about the history of the castle and its significance in Portuguese history.

Palaces

Pena Palace (Palácio da Pena)

Location: Sintra

Overview:

Pena Palace is a whimsical and colorful palace perched on a hilltop in Sintra. Commissioned by King Ferdinand II in the 19th century, this Romanticist palace blends various architectural styles, including Gothic, Manueline, Moorish, and Renaissance, creating a fairytale-like appearance.

Highlights:

- Wander through the palace's lavishly decorated rooms.
- Stroll through the lush gardens, filled with exotic plants and trees.
- Enjoy panoramic views of Sintra and the surrounding countryside from the palace terraces.

Queluz National Palace (Palácio Nacional de Queluz)

Location: Queluz

Overview:

Queluz National Palace is an exquisite example of 18th-century Portuguese architecture, often referred to as the "Portuguese Versailles." Originally a summer residence for the royal family, the palace is renowned for its Rococo and Baroque design and its beautifully landscaped gardens.

Highlights:

- Explore the opulent staterooms, including the Throne Room and the Music Room.
- Stroll through the formal gardens, featuring fountains, statues, and the impressive Robillion Pavilion.
- Visit the adjoining Queluz National Palace gardens, with their intricate designs and tranquil ambiance.

National Palace of Sintra (Palácio Nacional de Sintra)

Location: Sintra

Overview:

The National Palace of Sintra, also known as the Town Palace, is one of the best-preserved medieval royal residences in Portugal. Its distinctive twin chimneys and blend of Gothic, Manueline, and Moorish architectural styles make it a striking landmark in the heart of Sintra.

Highlights:

- Explore the richly decorated rooms, including the Swan Room and the Magpie Room.
- Discover the stunning azulejos (ceramic tiles) that adorn the palace walls.
- Learn about the palace's history and its role as a royal residence for centuries.

Fortresses

Belém Tower (Torre de Belém)

Location: Lisbon

Overview:

Belém Tower, a UNESCO World Heritage site, is an iconic fortress that stands at the mouth of the Tagus River. Built in the early 16th century to defend Lisbon's harbor, this Manueline masterpiece also served as a ceremonial gateway for Portuguese explorers during the Age of Discoveries.

Highlights:

- Climb to the top of the tower for views of the river and the surrounding area.

- Explore the tower's bastions and ornate battlements.

- Visit the dungeons and the King's Chamber.

Fort of São João Baptista (Forte de São João Baptista)

Location: Berlengas Islands

Overview:

Situated on the Berlengas Islands off the coast of Peniche, the Fort of São João Baptista is a remarkable example of military architecture adapted to a rugged, remote location. Built in the 17th century to protect against pirates and invaders, the fort is now a popular spot for visitors seeking adventure and history.

Highlights:

- Explore the fort's stone walls and bastions.
- Enjoy stunning views of the Atlantic Ocean and the surrounding islands.
- Learn about the fort's history and its strategic importance.

Sagres Fortress (Fortaleza de Sagres)

Location: Sagres

Overview:

Sagres Fortress, located on a dramatic promontory in the Algarve, is closely linked to Portugal's Age of Discoveries. It was from this point that Prince Henry the Navigator launched many of his exploratory voyages in the 15th century.

Highlights:

- Walk along the fortress walls and enjoy panoramic views of the coastline.
- Visit the Wind Rose (Rosa dos Ventos), a large stone compass believed to date back to the Age of Discoveries.
- Explore the lighthouse and learn about the maritime history of the area.

Portugal's castles, palaces, and fortresses are more than just architectural marvels; they are gateways to the past, offering insights into the country's rich history and cultural heritage.

Each structure, with its unique design and historical significance, tells a story of power, artistry, and resilience. Whether you're exploring the medieval ramparts of São Jorge Castle, the romantic halls of Pena Palace, or the strategic fortifications of Belém Tower, these landmarks provide a captivating journey through Portugal's storied past.

Natural Parks and Scenic Landscapes in Portugal

Portugal's natural beauty is as diverse as its cultural heritage. From rugged coastlines and serene valleys to lush forests and volcanic islands, the country's natural parks and scenic landscapes offer a wealth of outdoor experiences for nature lovers and adventure seekers. In this section, we will explore some of Portugal's most stunning natural parks and scenic landscapes, highlighting their unique features and the best ways to experience their beauty.

Peneda-Gerés National Park

Location: Northern Portugal

Overview:

Peneda-Gerês National Park, Portugal's only national park, is a vast and diverse natural area that spans the mountainous regions of Peneda, Gerês, and Soajo. Known for its breathtaking landscapes, rich biodiversity, and cultural heritage, this park is a paradise for hikers, wildlife enthusiasts, and history buffs.

Highlights:

- Hike through ancient forests, past cascading waterfalls, and along granite peaks.
- Explore traditional villages and the remains of Roman roads and bridges.
- Spot wildlife such as Iberian wolves, golden eagles, and wild ponies.

Douro Valley

Location: Northern Portugal

Overview:

The Douro Valley, a UNESCO World Heritage site, is renowned for its stunning terraced vineyards that produce the world-famous Port wine. The valley's scenic beauty, with the Douro River winding through steep hills covered in vines, offers a picturesque landscape that changes with the seasons.

Highlights:

- Take a river cruise to admire the terraced vineyards and charming Quintas (wine estates).
- Visit wine cellars to taste the region's acclaimed Port and table wines.
- Explore the quaint villages and historic towns that dot the valley.

Sintra-Cascais Natural Park

Location: Lisbon District

Overview:

Sintra-Cascais Natural Park combines dramatic coastal scenery with lush mountain landscapes. This protected area encompasses the fairytale palaces of Sintra, the rugged cliffs of Cabo da Roca, and the pristine beaches of Cascais, offering a diverse array of natural and cultural attractions.

Highlights:

- Discover the enchanting forests and gardens surrounding Pena Palace and Monserrate Palace.
- Visit Cabo da Roca, the westernmost point of mainland Europe, for stunning ocean views.

- Relax on the beautiful beaches of Guincho and Adraga, popular with surfers and sunbathers.

Arrábida Natural Park

Location: Setúbal Peninsula

Overview:

Arrábida Natural Park is known for its striking limestone cliffs, crystal-clear waters, and Mediterranean vegetation. This coastal park offers a peaceful retreat with its serene beaches, rich marine life, and scenic hiking trails.

Highlights:

- Hike through the park's hills for panoramic views of the Atlantic Ocean and the Setúbal Peninsula.
- Swim and snorkel in the turquoise waters of Portinho da Arrábida and Galápos Beach.

- Visit the historic Convent of Our Lady of Arrábida, nestled in the park's hills.

Ria Formosa Natural Park

Location: Algarve

Overview:
Ria Formosa Natural Park is a unique coastal lagoon system in the Algarve, known for its diverse birdlife and rich ecosystems. This protected area includes barrier islands, salt marshes, and tidal flats, making it a haven for birdwatchers and nature enthusiasts.

Highlights:
- Take a boat tour through the park's channels and lagoons to observe a variety of bird species, including flamingos and herons.

- Explore the picturesque islands of Culatra, Armona, and Farol, each offering beautiful beaches and tranquil settings.
- Learn about traditional salt production and the park's unique ecology at the visitor centers.

Madeira's Laurisilva Forest

Location: Madeira Island

Overview:

The Laurisilva Forest, a UNESCO World Heritage site, is an ancient laurel forest that covers much of Madeira's mountainous interior. This lush, misty forest is home to a rich array of endemic plant and animal species, making it a botanist's dream and a hiker's paradise.

Highlights:

- Hike along the levadas (irrigation channels) that crisscross the forest, offering stunning views and access to remote areas.

- Discover waterfalls, streams, and lush vegetation along the trails.

- Visit the Madeira Natural Park to learn about the conservation efforts and biodiversity of the Laurisilva Forest.

Azores' Sete Cidades

Location: São Miguel Island, Azores

Overview:

Sete Cidades is one of the most iconic and beautiful landscapes in the Azores. This volcanic caldera is home to twin lakes – Lagoa Azul and Lagoa Verde – surrounded by lush greenery and steep crater walls, creating a dramatic and serene setting.

Highlights:

- Drive to the Vista do Rei viewpoint for a breathtaking panorama of the twin lakes.

- Hike or bike around the crater rim and explore the tranquil paths leading down to the lakes.

- Enjoy the peaceful atmosphere and the stunning natural beauty of this unique volcanic landscape.

Vicentine Coast Natural Park

Location: Algarve and Alentejo

Overview:

The Vicentine Coast Natural Park stretches along the southwestern coast of Portugal, offering rugged cliffs, pristine beaches, and wild, unspoiled landscapes. This protected area is a haven for hikers, surfers, and nature lovers.

Highlights:

- Follow the Rota Vicentina trail, which offers some of the most scenic coastal hiking in Europe.

- Explore the secluded beaches and coves, such as Praia da Amoreira and Praia do Amado.
- Discover the charming fishing villages and traditional culture of the Alentejo and Algarve coasts.

Serra da Estrela Natural Park

Location: Central Portugal

Overview:
Serra da Estrela Natural Park is home to Portugal's highest mountain range, offering dramatic landscapes, glacial valleys, and unique flora and fauna. This park is a popular destination for hiking, skiing, and experiencing the great outdoors.

Highlights:
- Hike to the summit of Torre, the highest peak in mainland Portugal, for panoramic views.

- Discover the glacial valleys of Zêzere and Loriga, with their unique geological formations.
- Enjoy winter sports at the Serra da Estrela ski resort, or explore the park's trails in the warmer months.

Portugal's natural parks and scenic landscapes provide a diverse array of experiences for outdoor enthusiasts and nature lovers. From the lush forests of Madeira and the dramatic cliffs of the Algarve to the serene valleys of the Douro and the rugged beauty of the Vicentine Coast, these protected areas offer a glimpse into the country's remarkable natural heritage. Whether you seek adventure, relaxation, or simply a deeper connection with nature, Portugal's landscapes are sure to inspire and delight.

Beaches and Coastal Towns in Portugal

Portugal's coastline stretches over 1,100 miles, offering some of the most beautiful beaches and charming coastal towns in Europe. From the golden sands and dramatic cliffs of the Algarve to the wild, rugged shores of the Atlantic Coast, Portugal's beach destinations cater to every taste. Whether you're looking for world-class surf spots, tranquil coves, or lively seaside resorts, Portugal's beaches and coastal towns provide the perfect backdrop for a memorable holiday. In this section, we explore some of the best beaches and coastal towns that Portugal has to offer.

The Algarve

Praia da Marinha

Location: Lagos, Algarve

Overview:

Praia da Marinha is often considered one of the most beautiful beaches in the world. Known for its crystal-clear waters, striking limestone cliffs, and golden sands, this beach is a must-visit for anyone traveling to the Algarve.

Highlights:

- Snorkel in the clear waters to explore the rich marine life.
- Walk along the cliff-top trail for stunning views and photo opportunities.
- Relax on the sandy beach and enjoy the natural beauty.

Lagos

Overview:

Lagos is a vibrant town in the western Algarve known for its stunning beaches, historic center, and lively nightlife. It offers a mix of cultural attractions and beautiful coastal scenery.

Highlights:

- Visit Ponta da Piedade, famous for its dramatic rock formations and sea caves.
- Enjoy the sandy shores of Meia Praia, one of the longest beaches in the Algarve.
- Explore the historic center with its charming streets, shops, and restaurants.

Albufeira

Overview:

Albufeira is one of the most popular tourist destinations in the Algarve, known for its beautiful beaches, lively nightlife, and family-friendly attractions.

Highlights:

- Relax on the golden sands of Praia dos Pescadores, right in the heart of town.

- Explore the Old Town with its narrow streets, whitewashed buildings, and vibrant nightlife.

- Take a boat trip to explore the nearby sea caves and hidden beaches.

The Silver Coast (Costa de Prata)

Nazaré

Overview:

Nazaré is a picturesque fishing village famous for its giant waves and traditional character. It has become a hotspot for big-wave surfers from around the world.

Highlights:

- Watch surfers tackle some of the biggest waves in the world at Praia do Norte.
- Stroll along the beautiful sandy beach and enjoy fresh seafood at local restaurants.
- Visit the Sítio district for panoramic views and the Sanctuary of Our Lady of Nazaré.

Peniche

Overview:

Peniche is a renowned surf destination located on a rocky peninsula, offering excellent waves and a rich maritime history.

Highlights:

- Surf at Supertubos, one of the best surf breaks in Europe.

- Explore the historic Fort of Peniche, which now houses a museum.

- Take a boat trip to the Berlengas Islands, a natural reserve with crystal-clear waters and diverse marine life.

The Lisbon Coast

Cascais

Overview:

Cascais is a sophisticated coastal town near Lisbon, known for its beautiful beaches, elegant architecture, and vibrant cultural scene.

Highlights:

- Relax on Praia da Ribeira, a popular beach near the town center.
- Explore the charming streets of the historic center, filled with shops, cafes, and museums.
- Visit the stunning Boca do Inferno cliffs for breathtaking ocean views.

Estoril

Overview:

Estoril is a glamorous seaside town famous for its casino, beautiful beaches, and luxurious lifestyle.

Highlights:

- Spend a day at Tamariz Beach, a sandy beach with excellent facilities.

- Visit the Casino Estoril, one of the largest casinos in Europe.

- Enjoy the scenic promenade that stretches along the coast to Cascais.

The Alentejo Coast

Comporta

Overview:

Comporta is a serene and unspoiled destination on the Alentejo coast, known for its pristine beaches and rustic charm.

Highlights:

- Relax on the wide, sandy beaches such as Praia da Comporta and Praia do Pego.
- Explore the rice fields and traditional fishing villages in the surrounding area.
- Enjoy fresh seafood at beachside restaurants and cafes.

Vila Nova de Milfontes

Overview:

Vila Nova de Milfontes is a charming town situated at the mouth of the Mira River, offering beautiful beaches and a laid-back atmosphere.

Highlights:

- Relax on the sandy shores of Praia da Franquia and Praia das Furnas.
- Take a boat trip along the Mira River for scenic views and birdwatching.
- Explore the town's historic center and enjoy the local cuisine.

The North Coast

Porto

Overview:

Porto, Portugal's second-largest city, is not only known for its rich history and Port wine but also for its beautiful beaches located just a short distance from the city center.

Highlights:

- Visit Praia de Matosinhos, a popular beach for surfing and sunbathing.
- Explore the coastal promenade and enjoy fresh seafood at beachfront restaurants.
- Discover the historic Ribeira district and take a boat cruise on the Douro River.

Viana do Castelo

Overview:

Viana do Castelo is a picturesque coastal town in the Minho region, known for its stunning beaches and rich cultural heritage.

Highlights:

- Relax on the sandy beaches of Praia do Cabedelo and Praia da Amorosa.
- Explore the historic center with its beautiful architecture and vibrant atmosphere.
- Visit the Basilica of Santa Luzia for panoramic views of the coast and the town.

Portugal's beaches and coastal towns offer an incredible variety of experiences, from the golden sands and lively resorts of the Algarve to the wild, surf-friendly shores of the Silver Coast and the tranquil beauty of the Alentejo. Whether you're seeking adventure, relaxation, or cultural exploration, the coastal destinations of Portugal provide the perfect setting for an unforgettable holiday. From sunbathing and swimming to surfing and sightseeing, the beaches and towns of Portugal's coast are ready to welcome you with open arms.

Chapter 5

Experiencing Portuguese Culture

Portugal's rich and diverse culture is a reflection of its long history, geographical location, and the various civilizations that have influenced it over the centuries. Experiencing Portuguese culture involves delving into its traditions, music, cuisine, festivals, and everyday life. From the melancholic melodies of Fado music to the vibrant festivities that punctuate the calendar, Portuguese culture is warm, welcoming, and deeply rooted in its past. Here's an overview of the various facets of Portuguese culture that you can experience.

Fado Music

Overview:

Fado is the soul-stirring music of Portugal, characterized by its expressive and melancholic tunes. Originating in the 19th century in Lisbon, Fado is often performed in small taverns and cafes, creating an intimate and emotional atmosphere.

Highlights:

- Visit a Fado house in Lisbon or Porto to experience live performances.
- Learn about the history and significance of Fado at the Fado Museum in Lisbon.
- Listen to famous Fado singers like Amália Rodrigues, Mariza, and Carlos do Carmo.

Portuguese Cuisine

Overview:

Portuguese cuisine is a delightful blend of Mediterranean flavors, featuring fresh seafood, hearty meats, and a variety of spices. Each region boasts its own specialties, making Portugal a paradise for food lovers.

Highlights:

- Enjoy traditional dishes like Bacalhau à Brás (salted cod with potatoes and eggs), Caldo Verde (green soup), and Sardinhas Assadas (grilled sardines).
- Sample Pastéis de Nata (custard tarts) at the famous Pastéis de Belém bakery in Lisbon.
- Explore local markets such as Mercado da Ribeira in Lisbon and Mercado do Bolhão in Porto.

Wine and Port

Overview:

Portugal is renowned for its wines, particularly Port wine from the Douro Valley and Vinho Verde from the Minho region. Wine tasting is an integral part of experiencing Portuguese culture.

Highlights:

- Visit the wine cellars in Vila Nova de Gaia, across the river from Porto, to taste and learn about Port wine.
- Take a wine tour in the Douro Valley, one of the world's oldest wine regions.
- Explore the Alentejo region, known for its robust red wines and beautiful vineyards.

Festivals and Traditions

Overview:

Portugal's festivals and traditions are lively celebrations that reflect the country's cultural heritage and community spirit. These events are a great way to immerse yourself in local customs and festivities.

Highlights:

- Experience the Festa de São João in Porto, a midsummer festival featuring fireworks, music, and street parties.
- Celebrate Carnaval in cities like Lisbon, Ovar, and Torres Vedras with parades, costumes, and dancing.
- Attend the Festas dos Santos Populares in Lisbon, honoring saints with music, dance, and grilled sardines.

Portuguese Architecture

Overview:

Portugal's architecture is a testament to its rich history, showcasing a blend of Gothic, Manueline, Baroque, and modern styles. Exploring these architectural marvels is a journey through time.

Highlights:

- Visit the Jerónimos Monastery and Belém Tower in Lisbon, examples of Manueline architecture.
- Explore the historic city of Porto, with its Ribeira district and iconic Dom Luís I Bridge.
- Discover the palaces and castles of Sintra, including Pena Palace and the Moorish Castle.

Azulejos (Ceramic Tiles)

Overview:

Azulejos, the traditional ceramic tiles, are a distinctive feature of Portuguese art and architecture. These tiles, often painted in blue and white, adorn churches, palaces, and everyday buildings.

Highlights:

- Visit the National Tile Museum in Lisbon to see a vast collection of azulejos.
- Admire the tile work at São Bento Railway Station in Porto and the Igreja de São Vicente de Fora in Lisbon.
- Participate in a tile-painting workshop to create your own piece of Portuguese art.

Language and Literature

Overview:

Portuguese, the official language of Portugal, is spoken with a distinctive melody and rhythm. Portugal's literary heritage is rich, with notable contributions from poets, novelists, and playwrights.

Highlights:

- Read works by famous Portuguese authors such as Luís de Camões, Fernando Pessoa, and José Saramago.
- Visit the Fernando Pessoa House in Lisbon, dedicated to the life and works of the renowned poet.
- Explore the Bertrand Bookstore in Lisbon, the world's oldest operating bookstore.

Everyday Life and Social Etiquette

Overview:

Experiencing Portuguese culture also means understanding the nuances of everyday life and social interactions. The Portuguese are known for their hospitality, warmth, and relaxed lifestyle.

Highlights:

- Enjoy a leisurely meal at a local Tasca (tavern) and savor the unhurried pace of life.
- Engage in a café culture by spending time at traditional coffee shops, enjoying a bica (espresso) and a pastry.
- Respect local customs and etiquette, such as greeting with a handshake or cheek kisses and being punctual for social gatherings.

Experiencing Portuguese culture is a journey into the heart of a nation that cherishes its traditions, celebrates its history, and welcomes visitors with open arms. From the haunting strains of Fado music and the flavors of its cuisine to the grandeur of its architecture and the warmth of its people, Portugal offers a rich cultural tapestry that is both captivating and unforgettable. Whether you are exploring its vibrant cities, picturesque towns, or serene countryside, you will find that Portuguese culture is as diverse and inviting as the country itself.

Fado Music and Traditional Performances in Portugal

Fado, the soulful and emotive music of Portugal, is an integral part of the country's cultural heritage. With its haunting melodies, poignant lyrics, and expressive vocals, Fado captures the essence of Portuguese identity and emotion. Originating in the streets and taverns of Lisbon in the early 19th century, Fado has evolved into a cherished art form that continues to captivate audiences around the world. In this section, we delve into the origins, characteristics, and significance of Fado music, as well as traditional performances that showcase this unique cultural treasure.

Origins and Evolution of Fado

Overview:

Fado traces its roots to the working-class neighborhoods of Lisbon, particularly the Alfama district, where it emerged as a form of expression for sailors, fishermen, and marginalized communities. Influenced by African rhythms, Moorish melodies, and Portuguese folk music, Fado evolved into a genre known for its melancholic themes and passionate delivery.

Characteristics:

- Saudade: Central to Fado is the concept of "saudade," a Portuguese word that encapsulates a deep sense of longing, nostalgia, and melancholy.

- Guitarra Portuguesa: The traditional Portuguese guitar, with its distinctive pear-shaped body and twelve strings, is essential to the sound of Fado, providing a melodic accompaniment to the vocals.

- Themes: Fado lyrics often explore themes of love, loss, destiny, and the struggles of everyday life, reflecting the universal human experience.

Traditional Fado Performances

Fado Houses (Casas de Fado)

Overview:

Fado Houses, or "Casas de Fado," are intimate venues where audiences can experience live Fado performances in an authentic setting. These establishments range from small taverns to elegant restaurants, each offering a unique atmosphere and lineup of artists.

Highlights:

- Alfama District, Lisbon: Explore the historic Alfama neighborhood, home to some of the oldest and most renowned Fado Houses in Lisbon, such as "Clube de Fado" and "A Parreirinha de Alfama."

- Bairro Alto, Lisbon: Wander through the narrow streets of Bairro Alto to discover hidden gems like "Adega Machado" and "Sr. Fado de Alfama," where you can enjoy Fado performances alongside delicious Portuguese cuisine.

- Coimbra: Experience the distinctive style of Coimbra Fado, performed by students in the city's traditional "Repúblicas" and Fado Houses like "A Capella" and "Fado ao Centro."

Concert Halls and Theaters

Overview:

In addition to Fado Houses, Portugal's concert halls and theaters frequently host Fado performances featuring renowned artists and rising talents. These venues provide a larger stage for Fado artists to showcase their artistry and reach a wider audience.

Highlights:

- Coliseu dos Recreios, Lisbon: Attend concerts at this historic venue, which has hosted legendary Fado singers like Amália Rodrigues and Mariza.
- Casa da Música, Porto: enjoy Fado performances in the striking modern architecture of Casa da Música, one of Portugal's premier concert halls.
- Teatro José Lúcio da Silva, Leiria: Discover Fado artists from across Portugal at this cultural hub, which showcases a diverse range of performances.

Festivals and Events

Overview:

Festivals and events celebrating Fado are held throughout Portugal, offering opportunities to immerse yourself in the music and culture of Fado alongside locals and visitors alike. These gatherings showcase a wide array of Fado styles, from traditional to contemporary interpretations.

Highlights:

- Festival Internacional de Fado, Lisbon: Experience the world's largest Fado festival, featuring concerts, workshops, and competitions that celebrate the diversity of Fado music.

- Fado ao Centro Festival, Coimbra: Immerse yourself in Coimbra's rich Fado tradition at this annual festival, which brings together performers, scholars, and enthusiasts for a week of music and culture.

- Fado Fest, Porto: Discover emerging Fado artists and established performers at this dynamic festival, which highlights the vibrant Fado scene in Porto and the northern regions of Portugal.

Preserving and Promoting Fado

Overview:

Efforts to preserve and promote Fado as a cultural heritage have led to its inclusion on UNESCO's Representative List of the Intangible Cultural Heritage of Humanity. Organizations, institutions, and dedicated individuals play crucial roles in safeguarding Fado's legacy and ensuring its continued vitality for future generations.

Initiatives:

- Fado Museum (Museu do Fado), Lisbon: Explore the history, instruments, and legends of Fado at this museum, which offers exhibitions, workshops, and educational programs for visitors of all ages.

- Amália Rodrigues Foundation: Established in honor of the legendary Fado singer Amália Rodrigues, this foundation supports Fado artists, preserves archival materials, and promotes Fado internationally.

- Academia de Fado: Founded to educate and train aspiring Fado artists, the Academia de Fado offers courses, masterclasses, and performance opportunities to nurture talent and foster creativity.

Fado music is more than just a genre; it's a profound expression of Portuguese culture, history, and emotion. Whether you're listening to a haunting melody in a dimly lit tavern in Alfama or attending a grand concert in Lisbon's Coliseu dos Recreios, Fado has the power to transport you to the heart and soul of Portugal. Through its timeless themes and soul-stirring melodies, Fado continues to captivate audiences around the world, serving as a cherished symbol of Portuguese identity and heritage.

Culinary Delights: Port Wine, Pastries, and Seafood

Portugal's culinary landscape is a tantalizing fusion of flavors, influenced by its rich history, diverse landscapes, and maritime heritage. From the world-renowned Port wine to delectable pastries and fresh seafood dishes, Portuguese cuisine offers a feast for the senses. In this section, we explore some of Portugal's most iconic culinary delights, including Port wine, pastries, and seafood, and delve into the cultural significance and unique flavors that make them so beloved.

Port Wine

Overview:

Port wine, or simply Port, is one of Portugal's most famous exports and a symbol of the country's winemaking prowess. Produced exclusively in the Douro Valley region, Port is a fortified wine known for its rich flavors, deep colors, and sweet aromas.

Varieties:

- Ruby Port: Young and vibrant, with fruity flavors and a deep red color.
- Tawny Port: Aged in wooden barrels, resulting in nutty, caramelized notes and a lighter color.
- Vintage Port: Produced from the best grapes in exceptional years, offering intense flavors and complexity.

Highlights:

- Port Wine Cellars: Visit the historic wine cellars in Vila Nova de Gaia, across the Douro River from Porto, for guided tours and tastings.

- Douro River Cruises: Enjoy scenic boat tours along the Douro River, passing through vineyard-clad hillsides and picturesque villages.

- Wine Tastings: Sample a variety of Port wines at local wine bars, restaurants, and wine estates throughout Portugal.

Pastries

Overview:

Portuguese pastries, or "pastéis," are a delightful indulgence enjoyed by locals and visitors alike. From flaky custard tarts to almond-filled delights, Portugal's pastry shops offer a sweet symphony of flavors and textures.

Varieties:

- Pastéis de Nata: These iconic custard tarts, with their crispy pastry crusts and creamy custard fillings, are a must-try treat in Portugal.

- Pastéis de Belém: Originating from the Belém district of Lisbon, these custard tarts are renowned for their secret recipe, passed down through generations.

- Travesseiros: Almond-filled pastries from the town of Sintra, known for their light, flaky pastry, and sweet almond paste.

Highlights:

- Café Culture: Experience Portugal's café culture by enjoying pastries alongside a cup of freshly brewed coffee or a glass of Port wine.

- Pastry Shops: Visit local pastry shops and bakeries to sample a variety of traditional and contemporary pastries, often made with regional ingredients and time-honored techniques.

- Cooking Workshops: Learn the art of pastry-making from expert bakers and pastry chefs through hands-on cooking workshops and culinary classes.

Seafood

Overview:

With its long coastline and abundant marine resources, Portugal boasts a rich seafood tradition that is celebrated in its cuisine. From grilled sardines to hearty fish stews, seafood dishes in Portugal showcase the freshest catch of the day.

Varieties:

- Bacalhau: Salted codfish is a staple of Portuguese cuisine, prepared in a variety of ways, from Bacalhau à Brás (shredded cod with eggs and potatoes) to Bacalhau com Natas (codfish with cream).

- Sardinhas Assadas: Grilled sardines, seasoned with sea salt and olive oil, are a summertime favorite at festivals and seaside restaurants.

- Caldeirada de Peixe: This hearty fish stew, made with a variety of seafood such as fish, shrimp, and shellfish, is simmered with tomatoes, onions, and aromatic herbs.

Highlights:

- Seafood Markets: Explore local fish markets and seafood markets in coastal towns and cities, where you can select fresh fish, shellfish, and crustaceans for your own culinary creations.

- Fisherman's Feasts: Attend traditional festivals and celebrations, such as the Feast of Saint Anthony in Lisbon or the Festival do Marisco in Olhão, where you can savor a variety of seafood specialties prepared by local chefs.

- Seafood Restaurants: Dine at seafood restaurants and seafood taverns known as "marisqueiras," where you can enjoy a variety of seafood dishes, from grilled fish to seafood rice and shellfish platters.

Portugal's culinary delights, including Port wine, pastries, and seafood, offer a tantalizing glimpse into the country's rich gastronomic heritage. Whether you're sipping a glass of aged Port wine in a historic wine cellar, savoring a warm custard tart in a quaint pastry shop, or indulging in a seafood feast by the seaside, Portugal's flavors are sure to leave a lasting impression. From north to south, Portugal's culinary landscape is a celebration of tradition, innovation, and the bounty of land and sea. So, take a culinary journey through Portugal and savor the tastes and textures that make it a true gastronomic paradise.

Festivals and Celebrations in Portugal

Portugal is a land of vibrant festivities and cultural celebrations, where centuries-old traditions blend seamlessly with modern revelry. From colorful carnivals to solemn religious processions, Portugal's festivals offer a glimpse into the country's rich history, diverse heritage, and lively spirit. Whether you're joining in the revelry of a local fest or witnessing the pageantry of a national holiday, Portugal's festivals are sure to leave a lasting impression. In this section, we explore some of the most notable festivals and celebrations that define the Portuguese calendar.

Carnival

Overview:

Carnival in Portugal is a lively and colorful celebration held in the days leading up to Lent, typically in February or March. While each region has its own traditions and customs, Carnival is universally marked by parades, costumes, music, and dancing.

Highlights:

- Torres Vedras Carnival: Known for its humorous and satirical themes, the Carnival in Torres Vedras features elaborate floats, colorful costumes, and street parties that attract thousands of revelers.

- Ovar Carnival: Famous for its intricately designed costumes and themed floats, the Carnival in Ovar is a feast for the eyes, with parades, music, and traditional dances filling the streets.

- Loule Carnival: Considered one of the largest and most extravagant Carnivals in Portugal, the Carnival in Loule features elaborate processions, masked balls, and street entertainment that showcase the region's rich cultural heritage.

Holy Week (Semana Santa)

Overview:

Holy Week, or Semana Santa, is a solemn religious observance that takes place in the week leading up to Easter Sunday. Throughout Portugal, communities commemorate the Passion, Death, and Resurrection of Jesus Christ with processions, religious services, and traditional rituals.

Highlights:

- Braga: Experience the grandeur of Holy Week in Braga, where processions featuring ornate statues and religious icons wind through the historic streets, accompanied by prayers and hymns.

- Funchal: Witness the solemnity of Holy Week in Funchal, Madeira, where beautifully adorned floats depicting scenes from the Bible are paraded through the city, creating a mesmerizing spectacle.

- Évora: Attend the poignant Good Friday procession in Évora, featuring hooded penitents carrying crosses and statues as they make their way through the ancient streets of the city.

Saint Anthony's Festival (Festas de Santo António)

Overview:

Saint Anthony's Festival, held annually on June 12th and 13th, is one of Lisbon's most beloved celebrations. Honoring Saint Anthony, the patron saint of the city, the festival is marked by parades, street parties, and traditional music and dance.

Highlights:

- Sardine Barbecues: Join locals in the Alfama district for sardine barbecues, where the aroma of grilled fish fills the air and the streets come alive with music, dancing, and revelry.
- Wedding Ceremonies: Witness mock wedding ceremonies in which couples dress in traditional attire and exchange vows in a playful reenactment of Saint Anthony's role as the patron saint of marriage and matchmaking.
- Processions and Concerts: Experience the festive atmosphere of the festival with colorful processions, live

music performances, and fireworks displays that light up the night sky.

Saint John's Festival (Festas de São João)

Overview:

Saint John's Festival, celebrated on the night of June 23rd, is one of Portugal's most popular summer festivals. Rooted in ancient pagan traditions and Christian beliefs, the festival is marked by bonfires, street parties, and traditional rituals.

Highlights:

- Street Parties: Join the lively street parties in Porto, where revelers gather to dance, sing, and exchange "martelinhos" (small plastic hammers) as symbols of good luck.
- Fireworks: Watch spectacular fireworks displays lighting up the skies over Porto and other cities across Portugal, marking the culmination of the festival celebrations.

- Traditional Customs: Participate in traditional customs such as jumping over bonfires, releasing illuminated paper lanterns, and eating "caldo verde" (a traditional soup) with grilled sardines and cornbread.

Fátima Pilgrimage (Festa de Fátima)

Overview:

The Fátima Pilgrimage, held annually on May 13th, commemorates the apparitions of the Virgin Mary to three shepherd children in Fátima in 1917. Hundreds of thousands of pilgrims from around the world gather at the Sanctuary of Fátima to pray, attend Mass, and pay homage to Our Lady of Fátima.

Highlights:

- Candlelight Procession: Join the candlelight procession, in which pilgrims walk the "Via Sacra" (Sacred Way) carrying candles and praying the Rosary in procession around the sanctuary grounds.

- Mass Celebrations: Attend Mass at the Basilica of Our Lady of the Rosary, where the three shepherd children are buried, and participate in the solemn rituals and religious ceremonies that take place throughout the day.

- Vigil: Stay for the overnight vigil, joining fellow pilgrims in prayer and reflection as they await the dawn of a new day in the presence of Our Lady of Fátima.

Portugal's festivals and celebrations offer a colorful tapestry of traditions, rituals, and cultural expressions that showcase the country's vibrant spirit and rich heritage. Whether you're dancing in the streets during Carnival, witnessing the solemn processions of Holy Week, or joining the festivities of Saint Anthony's and Saint John's festivals, Portugal's festivals provide unforgettable experiences that celebrate life, faith, and community. So, immerse yourself in the sights, sounds, and flavors of Portugal's festivals, and discover the magic of this captivating country's cultural celebrations.

Art, Architecture, and Handicrafts in Portugal

Portugal boasts a rich cultural heritage that manifests vividly through its art, architecture, and handicrafts. From intricate azulejos to grandiose Manueline structures and exquisite hand-crafted goods, Portuguese creativity and craftsmanship reflect the country's history and diverse influences. This section explores the vibrant artistic landscape of Portugal, highlighting key elements of its art, architecture, and handicraft traditions.

Art

Azulejos

Overview:

Azulejos, the traditional Portuguese ceramic tiles, are one of the most iconic forms of art in Portugal. These tiles adorn the interiors and exteriors of buildings, creating stunning visual narratives through intricate designs and vibrant colors.

Highlights:

- National Tile Museum (Museu Nacional do Azulejo): Located in Lisbon, this museum showcases the history and artistry of azulejos from their origins to contemporary works.
- Public Spaces: Explore the beautiful azulejo murals at São Bento Railway Station in Porto and the Igreja de São Vicente de Fora in Lisbon.
- Workshops: Participate in azulejo-painting workshops to learn the techniques and create your own tile.

Painting and Sculpture

Overview:

Portuguese painting and sculpture have evolved through various artistic movements, from medieval religious art to contemporary works. Renowned Portuguese artists have contributed significantly to both national and international art scenes.

Highlights:

- Nuno Gonçalves: Known for the "Panels of Saint Vincent," a masterpiece of Portuguese art from the 15th century.
- Amadeo de Souza-Cardoso: A modernist painter whose work blends Cubism, Futurism, and Expressionism.
- Joana Vasconcelos: A contemporary artist recognized for her large-scale installations and sculptures.

Contemporary Art

Overview:

Portugal's contemporary art scene is dynamic and diverse, with numerous galleries, museums, and cultural spaces showcasing innovative works by modern artists.

Highlights:

- Berardo Collection Museum: Located in Lisbon, this museum houses an extensive collection of modern and contemporary art, including works by Warhol, Picasso, and Duchamp.

- MAAT (Museum of Art, Architecture, and Technology): A cutting-edge cultural institution in Lisbon that explores the intersection of art and technology.

- Serralves Museum of Contemporary Art: Situated in Porto, this museum features rotating exhibitions of contemporary art within a stunning modernist building and expansive gardens.

Architecture

Manueline Style

Overview:

The Manueline style, also known as Portuguese late Gothic, is a distinctive architectural style that emerged during the reign of King Manuel I (1495-1521). It combines Gothic elements with maritime motifs and symbols of the Age of Discoveries.

Highlights:

- Jerónimos Monastery: A UNESCO World Heritage site in Lisbon, renowned for its intricate Manueline details and historical significance.

- Belém Tower: Another UNESCO site, this fortified tower exemplifies Manueline architecture with its ornate stonework and maritime symbols.
- Batalha Monastery: A masterpiece of Gothic and Manueline architecture, featuring stunning cloisters and royal tombs.

Baroque and Rococo

Overview:
Baroque and Rococo architecture flourished in Portugal during the 17th and 18th centuries, characterized by ornate decorations, elaborate façades, and grandiose interiors.

Highlights:
- Palácio Nacional de Mafra: A monumental Baroque palace with an impressive basilica, convent, and royal apartments.
- Clérigos Tower: A Baroque bell tower in Porto, offering panoramic views of the city.

- São Roque Church: Located in Lisbon, this church boasts opulent Rococo interiors, including the lavish Chapel of St. John the Baptist.

Modern and Contemporary Architecture

Overview:

Portugal's architectural landscape continues to evolve, with contemporary architects creating innovative structures that blend tradition and modernity.

Highlights:

- Sapo '98 Pavilion (Pavilhão de Portugal): Designed by Álvaro Siza Vieira for the Lisbon World Exposition, this pavilion is a striking example of contemporary Portuguese architecture.

- Casa da Música: A concert hall in Porto designed by Rem Koolhaas, known for its bold design and acoustical excellence.

- EDP Headquarters: A cutting-edge office building in Lisbon, designed by Aires Mateus, featuring sustainable and innovative architectural solutions.

Handicrafts

Pottery and Ceramics

Overview:

Portugal has a rich tradition of pottery and ceramics, with each region producing unique styles and techniques. From decorative tiles to functional cookware, Portuguese ceramics are celebrated for their quality and artistry.

Highlights:

- Caldas da Rainha: Known for its whimsical and artistic ceramic pieces, including the iconic Bordallo Pinheiro tableware.

- São Pedro do Corval: A village in Alentejo renowned for its traditional pottery, where you can visit workshops and purchase handmade ceramics.
- Red Clay Pottery: Explore the red clay pottery of the Algarve, featuring distinctive shapes and earthy tones.

Embroidery and Textiles

Overview:

Portuguese embroidery and textiles are renowned for their intricate patterns and fine craftsmanship. Traditional techniques are passed down through generations, creating beautiful and functional works of art.

Highlights:

- Madeiran Embroidery: Delicate and intricate embroidery from the island of Madeira, often used for table linens, clothing, and decorative items.

- Arraiolos Rugs: Hand-embroidered wool rugs from the town of Arraiolos, featuring traditional geometric and floral designs.

- Linho de Viana: Linen textiles from Viana do Castelo, are known for their high quality and traditional motifs.

Basketry and Weaving

Overview:

Basketry and weaving are ancient crafts in Portugal, producing practical and decorative items from natural materials such as reed, wicker, and straw.

Highlights:

- Coimbra Baskets: Handwoven baskets from the Coimbra region, used for a variety of purposes, from carrying goods to home decor.

- Palm Leaf Weaving: Traditional palm leaf weaving in the Algarve, creating baskets, hats, and other items with intricate patterns.
- Esparto Grass Crafts: Esparto grass is used in the Alentejo region to create sturdy and functional items such as mats, bags, and footwear.

Portugal's rich cultural heritage is beautifully expressed through its art, architecture, and handicrafts. Whether admiring the intricate azulejos, exploring grand Manueline structures, or discovering unique handmade goods, visitors to Portugal are immersed in a world of creativity and craftsmanship. These artistic traditions not only reflect Portugal's history and influences but also continue to inspire and captivate, making the country a treasure trove of cultural experiences.

Chapter 6

Outdoor Adventures in Portugal

Portugal, with its diverse landscapes and mild climate, is a haven for outdoor enthusiasts. From the rugged mountains and verdant national parks to the stunning coastline and serene waterways, the country offers a wealth of activities for nature lovers and adventure seekers alike.

Hiking and Trekking

Explore Portugal's natural beauty on foot with its extensive network of hiking trails. Peneda-Gerês National Park, the country's only national park, offers dramatic landscapes, ancient forests, and scenic trails. The Rota Vicentina, along the southwest coast, provides breathtaking coastal views and a glimpse into rural life through the Fishermen's Trail and the Historical Way.

Surfing

Portugal is a world-renowned surfing destination with consistent waves and diverse surf spots. Ericeira, the first World Surfing Reserve in Europe, attracts surfers of all levels, while Nazaré is famous for its colossal waves, drawing big wave surfers from around the globe.

Cycling

Cycling enthusiasts can enjoy scenic routes such as the Ecopista do Dão, a gentle trail through the Dão Valley, and the Algarve Coast, offering a mix of coastal and inland routes. These paths traverse vineyards, forests, and picturesque towns, showcasing Portugal's varied landscapes.

Water Sports

Portugal's rivers, lakes, and coastline are perfect for kayaking, canoeing, and scuba diving. Paddle along the Douro River or the tranquil Alqueva Lake, or explore the Algarve's stunning sea caves. For underwater adventures, the clear waters of Madeira and the Azores offer excellent diving opportunities, teeming with marine life and volcanic formations.

Portugal's diverse natural settings provide a playground for outdoor activities, whether you're hiking, surfing, cycling, or exploring underwater. The country's scenic beauty and favorable climate make it an ideal destination for year-round outdoor adventures.

Hiking and Trekking Routes in Portugal

Portugal offers a plethora of hiking and trekking routes that showcase its diverse landscapes, from coastal cliffs and rolling hills to rugged mountains and lush forests. These trails provide opportunities to explore the natural beauty, cultural heritage, and rural charm of the country. Here are some of the most notable hiking and trekking routes in Portugal.

Peneda-Gerês National Park

Overview:

Peneda-Gerês National Park, located in the northwest of Portugal, is a hiker's paradise. It is the country's only national park and is known for its dramatic scenery, ancient forests, and rich biodiversity.

Key Trails:

- Trilho dos Currais: This circular trail offers panoramic views of the park's mountains, valleys, and rivers. It is a moderate hike, suitable for most fitness levels.

- Cascata do Arado to Pedra Bela: A route that leads to the impressive Arado Waterfall and the Pedra Bela viewpoint, providing stunning vistas of the surrounding landscape.

- Sistelo Village Trail: Known as the "Portuguese Tibet," this trail takes you through terraced fields and traditional villages, offering a glimpse into rural life.

Rota Vicentina

Overview:

The Rota Vicentina is a network of walking trails along the southwest coast of Portugal. It comprises two main routes: the Fishermen's Trail and the Historical Way, both offering breathtaking coastal scenery and charming inland paths.

Key Trails:

- Fishermen's Trail: Stretching from Porto Covo to Odeceixe, this rugged coastal path is ideal for those who love dramatic cliffs, secluded beaches, and traditional fishing villages. It is known for its challenging terrain and stunning ocean views.

- Historical Way: This inland trail runs from Santiago do Cacém to Cabo de São Vicente, passing through forests, rolling hills, and historic towns. It is less demanding than the Fishermen's Trail and offers a more tranquil hiking experience.

Madeira Island

Overview:

Madeira, a Portuguese archipelago in the Atlantic Ocean, is renowned for its lush landscapes, rugged mountains, and levadas (irrigation channels). The island offers numerous hiking trails that cater to various levels of difficulty.

Key Trails:

- Levada das 25 Fontes: One of Madeira's most popular hikes, this trail takes you through laurel forests to a stunning waterfall with 25 natural springs.

- Pico do Arieiro to Pico Ruivo: This challenging trail connects two of Madeira's highest peaks, offering spectacular views and diverse landscapes. It is a favorite among experienced hikers.

- Vereda da Ponta de São Lourenço: A relatively easy hike along the easternmost peninsula of Madeira, featuring dramatic coastal scenery and unique rock formations.

Serra da Estrela

Overview:

Serra da Estrela, the highest mountain range in mainland Portugal, offers a variety of hiking trails that showcase its granite peaks, glacial valleys, and alpine meadows.

Key Trails:

- Torre to Lagoa Comprida: This trail starts at Torre, the highest point in Serra da Estrela, and descends to Lagoa Comprida, a beautiful glacial lake. It offers stunning views and diverse flora.

- Covão da Ametade: A short but scenic trail that takes you through a glacial valley with lush vegetation and granite boulders. It is perfect for a leisurely hike.

- Poço do Inferno: This moderate trail leads to a picturesque waterfall known as Poço do Inferno, surrounded by verdant forests and rocky outcrops.

Azores Islands

Overview:

The Azores, an archipelago in the Atlantic Ocean, are known for their volcanic landscapes, lush greenery, and pristine lakes. The islands offer numerous hiking trails that highlight their natural beauty.

Key Trails:

- Sete Cidades (São Miguel): This iconic trail around the twin lakes of Sete Cidades offers breathtaking views of the caldera and the surrounding landscape. It is a must-visit for any hiker.
- Pico Mountain (Pico Island): The highest peak in Portugal, Pico Mountain offers a challenging hike with rewarding views from the summit. It is suitable for experienced hikers.

- Fajã da Caldeira de Santo Cristo (São Jorge): This trail takes you to a remote coastal lagoon, passing through lush vegetation and dramatic cliffs. It is a moderate hike with stunning scenery

Portugal's hiking and trekking routes offer something for everyone, from the dramatic coastal paths of the Rota Vicentina to the lush trails of Madeira and the rugged peaks of Serra da Estrela. Whether you're an experienced hiker seeking a challenging adventure or a casual walker looking for scenic beauty, Portugal's diverse landscapes provide endless opportunities for outdoor exploration. So lace up your hiking boots, hit the trails, and discover the natural wonders of Portugal.

Surfing and Water Sports in Portugal

Portugal's extensive coastline, diverse marine environments, and favorable weather conditions make it a premier destination for surfing and a variety of water sports. From the powerful waves of Nazaré to the tranquil waters of the Algarve, there are opportunities for every level of water enthusiast. Here is an overview of the best spots and activities for surfing and water sports in Portugal.

Surfing

Ericeira

Overview:

Ericeira, located about 35 kilometers north of Lisbon, is a world-renowned surfing destination and the first World Surfing Reserve in Europe. Known for its consistent waves and diverse surf spots, it attracts surfers from around the globe.

Highlights:

- Ribeira d'Ilhas: Famous for its long, peeling right-hand waves, ideal for intermediate and advanced surfers.

- Coxos: Considered one of the best waves in Portugal, Coxos offers powerful, fast-breaking waves suitable for experienced surfers.

- Foz do Lizandro: A versatile beach break with waves for all levels, making it a great spot for beginners and families.

Nazaré

Overview:

Nazaré, a coastal town north of Lisbon, is legendary for its colossal waves, which are some of the largest in the world. The underwater Nazaré Canyon funnels Atlantic swells into towering breakers, making it a hotspot for big wave surfing.

Highlights:

- Praia do Norte: Known for its record-breaking waves, this beach is a magnet for big wave surfers and home to the annual Nazaré Tow Surfing Challenge.

- Nazaré Lighthouse: Offers stunning views of the massive waves and a vantage point to watch surfers tackle these giants.

- Surf Schools: For those new to surfing, Nazaré has several surf schools offering lessons in safer, smaller conditions.

Peniche

Overview:

Peniche, situated on a peninsula about 90 kilometers north of Lisbon, is another top surfing destination in Portugal. It offers a variety of waves suitable for all levels, with consistent surf year-round.

Highlights:

- Supertubos: Known for its fast, barreling waves, Supertubos is one of the most famous surf spots in Europe and hosts international competitions.

- Baleal: A more beginner-friendly area with several surf schools and a variety of waves suitable for different skill levels.

- Consolação: Offers powerful right-hand reef breaks and is popular among experienced surfers.

Water Sports

Kayaking and Canoeing

Overview:

Portugal's rivers, lakes, and coastline provide excellent opportunities for kayaking and canoeing. Paddlers can explore serene waterways, hidden caves, and dramatic coastlines.

Highlights:

- Douro River: Kayak along the picturesque Douro River, passing terraced vineyards and historic villages, with the option to explore Porto.

- Alqueva Lake: Paddle on the calm waters of Alqueva Lake, the largest artificial lake in Europe, surrounded by the scenic Alentejo countryside.
- Algarve Coast: Discover the stunning sea caves, rock formations, and hidden beaches of the Algarve on a guided kayaking tour.

Scuba Diving and Snorkeling

Overview:

Portugal's diverse marine life and clear waters make it a fantastic destination for scuba diving and snorkeling. Dive sites range from underwater caves and shipwrecks to vibrant marine ecosystems.

Highlights:

- Madeira: Known for its crystal-clear waters and rich marine biodiversity, Madeira offers excellent diving sites, including the Garajau Marine Reserve.

- Azores: The Azores archipelago is a premier diving destination, with opportunities to see whale sharks, manta rays, and volcanic underwater landscapes.

- Berlengas Islands: Located off the coast of Peniche, these islands are a marine reserve with clear waters, abundant fish, and fascinating underwater caves.

Stand-Up Paddleboarding (SUP)

Overview:

Stand-up paddleboarding is a popular and accessible water sport in Portugal, suitable for all ages and skill levels. The calm waters of rivers, lakes, and some coastal areas provide ideal conditions for SUP.

Highlights:

- Lisbon Coast: Enjoy paddleboarding along the scenic coastline of Cascais and Estoril, with stunning views and calm waters.

- Algarve: Explore the Algarve's beautiful coastline, paddling through sea caves and along golden beaches.

- Douro River: Paddleboarding on the Douro River offers a unique perspective of Porto's historic waterfront and the surrounding vineyards.

Windsurfing and Kitesurfing

Overview:

Portugal's coastal winds and favorable conditions make it an excellent destination for windsurfing and kitesurfing.

Several spots along the coast cater to these adrenaline-pumping sports.

Highlights:

- Guincho Beach: Located near Cascais, Guincho Beach is famous for its strong winds and waves, making it a top spot for windsurfing and kitesurfing.

- Lagoa de Óbidos: A large lagoon near Peniche, ideal for kitesurfing and windsurfing, with steady winds and shallow waters.

- Viana do Castelo: Offers consistent winds and a variety of conditions, attracting wind and kitesurfers of all levels.

Portugal's extensive coastline and diverse aquatic environments provide a playground for surfing and water sports enthusiasts. Whether you're riding the giant waves of Nazaré, kayaking along the Algarve's stunning coast, diving in the crystal-clear waters of Madeira, or paddleboarding on the Douro River, Portugal offers a wealth of opportunities to enjoy the water. The country's favorable weather and variety of conditions make it an ideal destination for both seasoned water sports enthusiasts and beginners looking to try something new.

Cycling Tours and Trails in Portugal

Portugal's diverse landscapes, scenic routes, and favorable climate make it an ideal destination for cycling enthusiasts of all levels. From leisurely coastal rides to challenging mountain trails, there are cycling tours and routes to suit every preference. Explore the country's natural beauty, historic landmarks, and charming villages on two wheels with these top cycling tours and trails in Portugal.

Ecopista do Dão

Overview:

The Ecopista do Dão is a picturesque cycling trail that follows a former railway line through the Dão Valley in central Portugal. This 49-kilometer path offers a gentle ride through vineyards, forests, and along the Dão River.

Highlights:

- Starting Point: Begin your journey in the historic city of Viseu, known for its charming old town and impressive cathedral.

- Scenic Route: Cycle through the tranquil countryside, passing by vineyards, orchards, and traditional villages.

- Lagoa Azul: Stop at Lagoa Azul (Blue Lagoon), a scenic spot along the trail, perfect for a picnic or a refreshing swim.

- End Point: Conclude your ride in Santa Comba Dão, a picturesque town nestled along the banks of the Dão River.

Algarve Coast

Overview:

The Algarve region in southern Portugal offers a variety of cycling routes that showcase its stunning coastline, golden beaches, and charming villages. From leisurely coastal rides to challenging mountain trails, there are options for cyclists of all levels.

Highlights:

- Rota Vicentina Cycling Route: Explore the Algarve section of the Rota Vicentina, a long-distance walking and cycling trail that follows the coastline and offers breathtaking views of cliffs, beaches, and rural landscapes.

- Via Algarviana: Cycle through the interior of the Algarve on the Via Algarviana, a network of trails that traverse hills, valleys, and traditional villages, providing a glimpse into the region's rural life and cultural heritage.

- Tavira: Explore the charming town of Tavira by bike, known for its historic architecture, cobbled streets, and scenic waterfront.

Douro Valley

Overview:

The Douro Valley, famous for its terraced vineyards and stunning landscapes, offers scenic cycling routes along the riverbanks and through the rolling hills of northern Portugal.

Highlights:

- Cycling along the Douro River: Ride along the banks of the Douro River, passing by vineyards, olive groves, and picturesque villages, with breathtaking views of the valley.

- Wine Tasting: Stop at local wineries along the route to sample the region's renowned Port wines and enjoy traditional Portuguese cuisine.

- Historic Villages: Explore charming villages such as Pinhão, Peso da Régua, and São João da Pesqueira, known for their historic landmarks, hospitality, and scenic beauty.

Alentejo Region

Overview:

The Alentejo region in southern Portugal offers cyclists a unique opportunity to explore its vast plains, cork oak forests, and medieval towns on two wheels.

Highlights:

- Cycling the Alentejo Coast: Follow the coastal trails of the Alentejo, cycling through rugged cliffs, sandy beaches, and traditional fishing villages, with opportunities for birdwatching and beachside picnics.

- Historic Towns: Explore historic towns such as Évora, Monsaraz, and Elvas, known for their well-preserved architecture, ancient city walls, and cultural heritage sites.

- Cork Forests: Ride through the scenic cork oak forests of the Alentejo, home to unique flora and fauna, and learn about the region's cork industry and sustainable practices.

Portugal offers a diverse range of cycling tours and trails that cater to cyclists of all abilities and interests. Whether you prefer coastal routes with ocean views, mountain trails through vineyards and valleys, or cultural tours exploring historic towns and landmarks, there's a cycling adventure waiting for you in Portugal. So grab your bike, don your helmet, and embark on an unforgettable journey through the stunning landscapes and rich heritage of this beautiful country.

Golfing in Portugal

Portugal has established itself as one of Europe's premier golfing destinations, boasting a combination of world-class courses, stunning landscapes, and year-round sunshine. With a diverse range of courses designed by renowned architects, golfers of all levels can enjoy teeing off against the backdrop of coastal cliffs, rolling hills, and lush vineyards. Here's everything you need to know about golfing in Portugal.

Algarve: Golfing Paradise

Overview:

The Algarve region, located in southern Portugal, is synonymous with golfing excellence. With over 40 courses scattered along its coastline, the Algarve offers golfers an unparalleled variety of playing experiences, from championship courses to scenic resort layouts.

Key Destinations:

- Vilamoura: Home to some of Portugal's most prestigious courses, including the Dom Pedro Victoria Golf Course, designed by Arnold Palmer, and the Old Course, one of the oldest in the region.

- Quinta do Lago: A golfing mecca boasting three championship courses—North, South, and Laranjal—set amidst the stunning Ria Formosa Natural Park.

- Vale do Lobo: Famous for its Royal and Ocean courses, which offer breathtaking sea views and challenging holes, including the iconic cliff-top 16th hole on the Royal Course.

Lisbon: Urban Elegance meets Golfing Excellence

Overview:

The Lisbon region combines cosmopolitan charm with exceptional golfing opportunities. With courses set against the backdrop of historic landmarks, scenic coastlines, and rolling countryside, Lisbon offers a unique golfing experience.

Key Destinations:

- Belas Clube de Campo: Located just outside Lisbon, this championship course winds its way through a picturesque landscape of valleys, lakes, and ancient trees.

- Penha Longa Resort: Set within the Sintra-Cascais Natural Park, this luxury resort features two championship courses—the Atlantic and the Monastery—designed by Robert Trent Jones Jr.

- Oitavos Dunes: Considered one of the finest links courses in Europe, Oitavos Dunes offers golfers a challenging and scenic layout overlooking the Atlantic Ocean.

Porto and the North: Golfing Gems in Northern Portugal

Overview:

Northern Portugal may be lesser known for its golfing offerings, but it boasts several hidden gems that are sure to delight golf enthusiasts. With courses nestled amidst vineyards, forests, and river valleys, Porto and the North offer a unique golfing experience.

Key Destinations:

- Estela Golf Club: Situated along the stunning Costa Verde, Estela Golf Club is renowned for its challenging links-style layout and panoramic ocean views.

- Vidago Palace Golf Course: Located near the historic town of Chaves, this scenic course meanders through a century-old park and offers a blend of parkland and woodland holes.

- Axis Golf Ponte de Lima: Designed by Arnold Palmer, this championship course in Ponte de Lima is set amidst vineyards and offers golfers a challenging yet enjoyable round.

Madeira and the Azores: Island Golfing Escapes

Overview:

For a truly unforgettable golfing experience, consider a trip to the islands of Madeira and the Azores. These volcanic archipelagos boast stunning landscapes, mild climates, and unique courses that will captivate golfers of all levels.

Key Destinations:

- Palheiro Golf: Set on the hills above Funchal, Madeira, this scenic course offers breathtaking views of the city and the Atlantic Ocean, along with challenging holes amidst lush vegetation.

- Furnas Golf Course: Located on São Miguel, the largest island in the Azores, this picturesque course is set within a volcanic crater and features natural hot springs, lakes, and lush vegetation.

- Batalha Golf Course: Situated on the island of Terceira, this challenging course winds its way through forests, meadows, and lava fields, offering stunning views of the Atlantic Ocean and the surrounding landscape.

Whether you're seeking championship challenges, scenic coastal layouts, or island escapes, Portugal offers a golfing experience like no other. With a diverse range of courses set amidst stunning landscapes and a welcoming climate year-round, Portugal has earned its reputation as a top golfing destination in Europe. So pack your clubs, book your tee times, and prepare for an unforgettable golfing adventure in Portugal.

Chapter 7

Eating and Drinking in Portugal

Portugal's rich culinary heritage is a reflection of its diverse history, varied landscapes, and cultural influences. From fresh seafood and hearty stews to world-renowned wines and delectable pastries, Portugal offers a gastronomic journey that delights the senses. Here's a guide to some of the must-try dishes, drinks, and dining experiences in this flavorful country.

Traditional Portuguese Dishes

Seafood Delicacies

Bacalhau (Salted Codfish):

Often called the national dish, bacalhau is prepared in numerous ways, with recipes claiming over 365 variations—one for each day of the year. Popular versions include Bacalhau à Brás (shredded cod with onions, potatoes, and eggs) and Bacalhau com Natas (cod baked with cream).

Sardinhas Assadas (Grilled Sardines):

A summertime favorite, grilled sardines are typically seasoned with olive oil and salt, and then cooked over open flames. They are often served with a side of roasted potatoes or fresh salad.

Polvo à Lagareiro (Octopus with Olive Oil and Garlic): Tender octopus baked with potatoes, garlic, and copious amounts of olive oil, this dish is a true representation of Portugal's love for simple, flavorful seafood.

Meat and Poultry

Cozido à Portuguesa:

A traditional meat stew featuring a mix of beef, pork, chicken, sausages, and vegetables. It's a hearty, comforting dish often enjoyed during colder months.

Frango Piri-Piri (Piri-Piri Chicken):

Spicy and flavorful, this dish features grilled chicken marinated with piri-piri sauce—a fiery concoction of chili peppers, garlic, and olive oil. It's a favorite in the Algarve region.

Pastries and Desserts

Pastéis de Nata (Custard Tarts):

Perhaps the most famous Portuguese dessert, these flaky pastry tarts filled with creamy custard are best enjoyed fresh from the oven. They are particularly renowned in Lisbon, where the pastéis from Pastéis de Belém are legendary.

Bolo de Bolacha (Portuguese Biscuit Cake):

A no-bake cake made with layers of coffee-soaked biscuits and a buttery cream filling, often topped with crushed cookies or chocolate.

Regional Specialties

Francesinha (Porto):

A hearty sandwich from Porto, the francesinha consists of layers of cured meats, steak, and sausage, covered with melted cheese and a rich tomato-beer sauce, often served with fries.

Cataplana de Marisco (Algarve):

A seafood stew cooked in a traditional cataplana (clam-shaped copper pot), featuring a mix of shellfish, fish, tomatoes, and bell peppers. It's a flavorful dish that captures the essence of the Algarve coast.

Caldo Verde (Minho):

A simple yet delicious soup made with kale, potatoes, and chouriço (smoked sausage), often served with a slice of cornbread.

Portuguese Wines and Beverages

Wines

Port Wine:

Produced exclusively in the Douro Valley, port wine is a fortified wine available in various styles, from sweet red ports to dry white ports. It's traditionally enjoyed as a dessert wine.

Vinho Verde:

Meaning "green wine," this young wine hails from the Minho region. It's light, fresh, and slightly effervescent, making it perfect for warm weather.

Douro Wines:

The Douro Valley is also known for its robust red wines, made from grape varieties such as Touriga Nacional. These wines are rich, full-bodied, and age well.

Beverages

Ginjinha:

A cherry liqueur made by infusing ginja berries in alcohol and adding sugar. It's typically served in small shot glasses, sometimes with a piece of fruit at the bottom.

Licor Beirão:

A popular herbal liqueur with a sweet, aromatic flavor, often enjoyed as a digestif.

Dining Etiquette and Tips

Dining Out

- Tascas and Adegas: For an authentic dining experience, visit a tasca (traditional tavern) or adega (wine cellar). These establishments offer hearty, home-cooked meals and a warm, convivial atmosphere.
- Petiscos: The Portuguese equivalent of tapas, petiscos are small plates meant for sharing. They include a variety of dishes like grilled chouriço, octopus salad, and cheese.

Eating Customs

- Meal Times: Lunch is typically served between 12:30 PM and 3:00 PM, while dinner is eaten later, often starting around 8:00 PM. It's common to have a mid-morning snack and a late afternoon coffee break.
- Cover Charges: In many restaurants, you may be served bread, olives, cheese, or other small starters before your meal. These are not free; they will be added to your bill if you consume them.

Eating and drinking in Portugal is an immersive experience that reflects the country's rich cultural heritage and diverse landscapes. Whether you're indulging in a seafood feast along the coast, savoring traditional meat dishes in the countryside, or enjoying a glass of port in the Douro Valley, Portugal offers a culinary journey that is sure to delight food lovers and wine enthusiasts alike.

Dining Spots in Portugal: From Casual Eateries to Gourmet Delights

When it comes to dining out in Portugal, there's no shortage of options to tantalize your taste buds. From cozy taverns serving up traditional fare to upscale restaurants showcasing innovative cuisine, Portugal offers a diverse culinary landscape that caters to every palate and occasion. Here are some dining spots worth exploring during your visit:

1. Tascas and Petiscarias

Overview:

Tascas and petiscarias are traditional Portuguese eateries known for their casual atmosphere and hearty, home-style cooking. These establishments serve a variety of petiscos (small plates), allowing diners to sample a wide range of flavors in a relaxed setting.

Key Spots:

- Adega São Nicolau (Lisbon): A charming Tasca in the heart of Lisbon's Alfama district, known for its cozy ambiance and authentic Portuguese dishes.
- Adega do Alentejano (Porto): This rustic tavern in Porto specializes in Alentejo cuisine, offering hearty stews, grilled meats, and regional wines.

2. Seafood Restaurants

Overview:

Given Portugal's extensive coastline, it's no surprise that seafood plays a prominent role in the country's culinary scene. Seafood restaurants abound, serving up fresh catches from the Atlantic Ocean prepared in a variety of delicious ways.

Key Spots:

- Ramiro (Lisbon): A beloved institution in Lisbon, Ramiro is renowned for its fresh seafood, including grilled tiger prawns, garlic shrimp, and crab.
- O Gaveto (Porto): Located in Matosinhos, O Gaveto is a seafood lover's paradise, offering a wide selection of fish and shellfish dishes in a lively atmosphere.

3. Michelin-Starred Restaurants

Overview:

For a truly exceptional dining experience, consider visiting one of Portugal's Michelin-starred restaurants. These establishments are known for their exquisite cuisine, impeccable service, and elegant ambiance.

Key Spots:

- Belcanto (Lisbon): Helmed by chef José Avillez, Belcanto is Lisbon's only two-Michelin-starred restaurant, offering contemporary Portuguese cuisine with a creative twist.
- The Yeatman (Porto): Situated in a luxury wine hotel overlooking the Douro River, The Yeatman boasts a Michelin-starred restaurant helmed by chef Ricardo Costa, known for its innovative dishes and extensive wine list.

4. Pastelarias and Confeitarias

Overview:

No visit to Portugal is complete without indulging in the country's delectable pastries and desserts. Pastelarias and confeitarias are pastry shops and bakeries where you can sample a wide array of sweet treats, from custard tarts to almond cakes.

Key Spots:

- Pastéis de Belém (Lisbon): A Lisbon institution since 1837, Pastéis de Belém is famous for its iconic custard tarts, known as pastéis de nata, which are baked according to a secret recipe passed down through generations.
- Casa Lapão (Porto): This historic confeitaria in Porto is renowned for its selection of traditional Portuguese pastries, including the decadent bolo de São Roque (Saint Roch cake) and the iconic ovos moles (sweet egg yolks).

5. Wine Bars and Cellars

Overview:

Portugal is celebrated for its wine production, with a rich heritage of winemaking dating back centuries. Wine bars and cellars offer the perfect opportunity to sample

Portugal's finest wines, from crisp Vinho Verde to full-bodied Douro reds.

Key Spots:

- By the Wine (Lisbon): Located in Lisbon's historic Chiado district, By the Wine is a stylish wine bar housed in a former chapel, offering an extensive selection of Portuguese wines by the glass or bottle.
- Graham's Port Lodge (Porto): Situated in Vila Nova de Gaia, across the river from Porto, Graham's Port Lodge offers guided tours and tastings of its renowned Port wines, with sweeping views of the Douro Valley.

From quaint tascas serving up traditional fare to Michelin-starred restaurants pushing the boundaries of culinary innovation, Portugal offers a dining scene that caters to every taste and budget. Whether you're craving fresh seafood, indulgent pastries, or world-class wines, you'll find plenty to satisfy your appetite in this gastronomic paradise.

So, venture out and explore the vibrant dining spots that Portugal has to offer, and prepare to embark on a culinary journey you won't soon forget.

Best Dishes to Try in Portugal: A Culinary Adventure

Portugal's rich culinary heritage is celebrated worldwide for its diverse flavors, fresh ingredients, and traditional recipes passed down through generations. From hearty stews and grilled seafood to delectable pastries and savory snacks, Portuguese cuisine offers a mouthwatering array of dishes that reflect the country's cultural diversity and coastal abundance. Here are some of the best dishes to try during your culinary adventure in Portugal:

1. Bacalhau à Brás

Overview:

Bacalhau à Brás is a quintessential Portuguese dish made with salted cod, onions, potatoes, eggs, and olives. The cod is shredded and sautéed with onions and garlic, then mixed with thinly sliced potatoes and scrambled eggs. It's often garnished with parsley and black olives, creating a flavorful and satisfying meal.

2. Caldo Verde

Overview:

Caldo Verde is a comforting kale and potato soup that's beloved throughout Portugal. Made with thinly sliced potatoes, shredded kale, onions, garlic, and Portuguese chouriço (sausage), this hearty soup is simmered until the flavors meld together. It's typically served with a drizzle of olive oil and crusty bread for dipping.

3. Pastéis de Nata

Overview:

Pastéis de Nata, also known as Portuguese custard tarts, are iconic pastries that originated in Lisbon. These delectable treats feature a flaky pastry crust filled with a creamy custard made from eggs, sugar, and milk. They're often dusted with cinnamon and powdered sugar before serving, creating a perfect balance of sweetness and spice.

4. Francesinha

Overview:

Francesinha is a hearty sandwich that hails from the city of Porto. It's made with layers of cured meats, such as ham, linguiça (smoked sausage), and steak, sandwiched between slices of bread. The sandwich is then topped with melted cheese and smothered in a rich and spicy tomato and beer sauce. It's typically served with a fried egg on top and a side of french fries.

5. Arroz de Marisco

Overview:

Arroz de Marisco, or seafood rice, is a beloved Portuguese dish that highlights the country's abundant seafood. It's made by simmering rice with a variety of shellfish, such as shrimp, clams, mussels, and crab, in a flavorful broth made with tomatoes, onions, garlic, and herbs. The result is a fragrant and satisfying dish that's perfect for seafood lovers.

6. Cozido à Portuguesa

Overview:

Cozido à Portuguesa is a traditional Portuguese stew that's often enjoyed during festive occasions and family gatherings. It features a variety of meats, such as pork, beef, chicken, and chorizo, as well as vegetables like potatoes, carrots, and cabbage. The stew is slow-cooked until the meats are tender and the flavors are melded together, resulting in a hearty and flavorful dish.

7. Sardinhas Assadas

Overview:

Sardinhas Assadas, or grilled sardines, is a summertime staple in Portugal, especially during the popular festivals known as Santos Populares. The fresh sardines are seasoned with salt and grilled over an open flame until crispy and golden brown. They're typically served with boiled potatoes, grilled peppers, and a squeeze of lemon, creating a simple yet delicious meal.

Portugal's culinary scene is a treasure trove of delicious dishes that showcase the country's rich cultural heritage and coastal bounty. From iconic specialties like Bacalhau à Brás and Pastéis de Nata to hearty stews and grilled seafood, there's something to satisfy every craving in Portugal. So, don't miss the opportunity to embark on a culinary adventure and indulge in the best dishes that Portugal has to offer. Your taste buds will thank you!

Chapter 8

Practical Information

Traveling to Portugal promises a rich tapestry of experiences, from its historic cities and stunning landscapes to its delectable cuisine and vibrant culture. However, to make the most of your journey, it's crucial to arm yourself with some practical information. This chapter serves as your essential guide to navigating the logistical aspects of your trip. From understanding the intricacies of transportation and communication to staying safe and healthy, and managing your finances, we cover all the necessary details to ensure a smooth and enjoyable stay in Portugal. Whether you're a seasoned traveler or embarking on your first international adventure, these insights will help you travel confidently and make the most of every moment in this captivating country.

Accommodation Options: Hotels, Pousadas, and Guesthouses

When planning your stay in Portugal, you'll find a wide range of accommodation options to suit every preference and budget. Whether you're looking for luxurious hotels, charming pousadas, or cozy guesthouses, Portugal offers a variety of places to rest and recharge after a day of exploring. Here's a guide to the different types of accommodations you can choose from:

Hotels

Overview:

Hotels in Portugal range from budget-friendly to high-end luxury, offering a variety of amenities and services to cater to different needs. They are typically rated by stars, with five-star hotels providing the most upscale experience.

Types of Hotels:

- Luxury Hotels: These offer top-notch amenities, including fine dining restaurants, spa services, and exquisite rooms with stunning views. Notable examples include the Four Seasons Hotel Ritz Lisbon and The Yeatman in Porto.

- Boutique Hotels: Smaller and more personalized, boutique hotels provide a unique and stylish experience. They often feature themed decor and are located in trendy or historic areas. Examples include Memmo Alfama in Lisbon and Torel Avantgarde in Porto.

- Budget Hotels: These are perfect for travelers looking for basic yet comfortable accommodations at an affordable price. Chains like Ibis and B&B Hotels have locations throughout the country.

Amenities:

- Free Wi-Fi

- Room service

- On-site restaurants and bars

- Fitness centers and swimming pools

- Concierge services

Pousadas

Overview:

Pousadas are a unique Portuguese accommodation option that blends history, culture, and luxury. Often housed in historic buildings such as castles, monasteries, and palaces, pousadas offer a distinctive and memorable stay.

Types of Pousadas:

- Historic Pousadas: These are located in significant historical buildings and provide a glimpse into Portugal's rich past. Examples include Pousada de Óbidos, housed in a medieval castle, and Pousada de Estremoz, situated in a 13th-century palace.

- Nature Pousadas: Located in scenic natural settings, these pousadas offer tranquility and beautiful landscapes. Pousada de Sagres, overlooking the Atlantic Ocean, and Pousada de Viseu, set in a converted hospital, are prime examples.

Amenities:

- Luxurious rooms with historical charm
- Gourmet restaurants serving local cuisine
- Beautifully landscaped gardens and courtyards
- Access to cultural and historical sites
- Personalized service and exclusive tours

Guesthouses

Overview:

Guesthouses, or "casas de hóspedes," provide a more intimate and homely atmosphere compared to hotels. They are often family-run and offer a personal touch that makes for a warm and welcoming stay.

Types of Guesthouses:

- Bed and Breakfasts (B&Bs): These typically include a comfortable room and a hearty breakfast. They are ideal for travelers seeking a cozy, home-like environment. Examples include Casa do Bairro in Lisbon and Casa dos Loios in Porto.

- Farm Stays (Agroturismo): Offering a rural retreat, farm stays allow guests to experience the countryside and often involve farm activities. Quinta da Pacheca in the Douro Valley and Herdade do Touril in Alentejo are popular choices.

- City Guesthouses: Located in urban areas, these guesthouses provide easy access to city attractions and amenities. They often feature charming decor and personalized service. Examples include Casa do Patio in Lisbon and 6Only Guest House in Porto.

Amenities:

- Personalized service and local recommendations
- Homemade breakfast and sometimes other meals
- Cozy, individually decorated rooms
- Common areas for socializing with other guests
- Often located in charming neighborhoods

Portugal's diverse accommodation options ensure that every traveler can find the perfect place to stay, whether it's the luxurious comfort of a high-end hotel, the historical charm of a pousada, or the cozy warmth of a guesthouse. By choosing accommodations that match your preferences and travel style, you can enhance your overall experience and enjoy the unique hospitality that Portugal has to offer.

Dining and Nightlife Recommendations

Portugal's vibrant dining and nightlife scenes are integral parts of the country's cultural fabric, offering a delightful mix of traditional flavors, contemporary cuisine, lively bars, and trendy nightclubs. Whether you're a foodie looking to savor authentic Portuguese dishes or a night owl eager to experience the local nightlife, Portugal has something to offer. Here are some recommendations to help you make the most of your dining and nightlife experiences.

Dining Recommendations

Traditional Portuguese Cuisine

1. A Cevicheria (Lisbon)

- Overview: A Cevicheria, located in the trendy Príncipe Real neighborhood, offers a modern take on Portuguese and South American seafood dishes. Renowned for its ceviche, the restaurant blends traditional Portuguese ingredients with innovative techniques.

- Must-Try: Try the classic Portuguese ceviche, which includes codfish, sweet potato, and corn.

2. O Paparico (Porto)

- Overview: O Paparico is a charming, rustic restaurant in Porto known for its authentic Portuguese dishes and warm hospitality. The restaurant's interior, adorned with traditional decor, creates an inviting atmosphere.
- Must-Try: The octopus rice and the suckling pig are highly recommended.

Contemporary and Fusion Cuisine

3. Belcanto (Lisbon)

- Overview: Helmed by Michelin-starred chef José Avillez, Belcanto offers a fine dining experience that combines traditional Portuguese flavors with modern culinary techniques. Located in Lisbon's Chiado district, it's perfect for a special night out.
- Must-Try: The "Garden of the Goose that Laid the Golden Eggs" dish is a standout.

4. The Yeatman (Porto)

- Overview: This Michelin-starred restaurant, located in a luxury wine hotel, offers breathtaking views of Porto and an exceptional dining experience. The menu focuses on innovative dishes that highlight Portuguese ingredients.
- Must-Try: The tasting menu with wine pairings showcases the best of Portuguese cuisine.

Casual and Budget-Friendly Options

5. Time Out Market (Lisbon)

- Overview: Located in the Mercado da Ribeira, Time Out Market brings together some of Lisbon's best restaurants and chefs under one roof. It's a great spot to sample a variety of dishes in a lively, market-style setting.
- Must-Try: Don't miss the pastéis de nata from Manteigaria.

6. Casa Guedes (Porto)

- Overview: Famous for its roast pork sandwiches, Casa Guedes is a popular spot for locals and tourists alike. It's an excellent choice for a quick, delicious, and affordable meal.
- Must-Try: The roast pork sandwich with Serra da Estrela cheese.

Nightlife Recommendations

Bars and Lounges

1. Pensão Amor (Lisbon)

- Overview: Once a brothel, Pensão Amor is now one of Lisbon's most eclectic bars. Located in the Cais do Sodré district, it features a quirky decor with multiple rooms, each with its unique ambiance.
- Highlights: Enjoy cocktails in the bar's vintage, bohemian atmosphere.

2. The Royal Cocktail Club (Porto)

- Overview: This stylish cocktail bar in Porto's downtown area offers expertly crafted drinks in a sophisticated setting. It's a perfect spot for a pre-dinner drink or a nightcap.
- Highlights: Try their signature cocktails and enjoy the elegant, old-world charm.

Live Music and Fado Houses

3. Clube de Fado (Lisbon)

- Overview: For an authentic fado experience, visit Clube de Fado in Lisbon's Alfama district. The intimate setting, combined with soulful performances, makes for an unforgettable evening.
- Highlights: Savor traditional Portuguese dishes while listening to live fado music.

4. Casa da Mariquinhas (Porto)

- Overview: This fado house in Porto offers a cozy atmosphere where you can enjoy traditional fado performances. The venue provides a genuine cultural experience with heartfelt music.
- Highlights: Pair the fado music with a selection of Portuguese wines.

Nightclubs

5. Lux Frágil (Lisbon)

- Overview: One of Lisbon's most famous nightclubs, Lux Frágil offers multiple floors of music, ranging from electronic and house to indie and rock. It also boasts a rooftop terrace with stunning views of the Tagus River.
- Highlights: Dance the night away to sets by top DJs and enjoy the vibrant atmosphere.

6. Plano B (Porto)

- Overview: Located in Porto's nightlife district, Plano B is a multi-level club with various rooms offering different music genres, from electronic and hip-hop to rock and funk. It's a favorite among locals and tourists.
- Highlights: Explore the club's different rooms and enjoy the eclectic music offerings.

Portugal's dining and nightlife scenes are as diverse and exciting as the country itself. From savoring traditional dishes in cozy tascas to experiencing the vibrant nightlife in trendy bars and clubs, there's something for everyone. Whether you're planning a romantic dinner, a casual meal, or a night out on the town, these recommendations will help you discover the best that Portugal has to offer.

Transportation: Getting Around by Train, Bus, and Car

Exploring Portugal's diverse landscapes, historic cities, and charming towns is a rewarding experience, made easier by the country's well-developed transportation network. Whether you prefer the convenience of trains, the flexibility of buses, or the freedom of driving, there are various options to suit your travel style and itinerary. Here's an overview of the primary modes of transportation in Portugal:

By Train

Overview:

Portugal's railway system is operated by Comboios de Portugal (CP), offering an extensive network that connects major cities, towns, and some rural areas. Trains are a comfortable and scenic way to travel, especially for longer distances.

Types of Trains:

- Alfa Pendular: The fastest and most comfortable option, Alfa Pendular trains connect major cities like Lisbon, Porto, Faro, and Braga. These trains offer first and second-class seating, Wi-Fi, and a dining car.

- Intercidades: These intercity trains are slightly slower than Alfa Pendular but still provide efficient service between major destinations. They offer both first and second-class seating.

270

- Regional and InterRegional: These trains connect smaller towns and rural areas, making more frequent stops. They are ideal for exploring less touristy parts of Portugal.

- Urban Trains: Serving metropolitan areas like Lisbon and Porto, urban trains are perfect for short commutes within the city and its suburbs.

Advantages:

- Comfort: Spacious seating and onboard amenities.
- Scenic Routes: Enjoy picturesque views of the countryside and coastline.
- Punctuality: Generally reliable and on time.

Tickets:

- Purchasing: Tickets can be bought online, at stations, or through the CP mobile app. It's advisable to book in advance for long-distance trains.
- Discounts: CP offers discounts for advance bookings, seniors, students, and families.

By Bus

Overview:

Buses in Portugal are a versatile and cost-effective way to travel, especially to destinations not served by trains. The bus network is extensive, covering cities, towns, and rural areas.

Types of Buses:

- Rede Expressos: This is the main long-distance bus service, connecting major cities and towns across the country. Buses are modern, with comfortable seating and onboard Wi-Fi.

- FlixBus: An international bus service that also operates within Portugal, offering affordable fares and extensive routes.

- Local and Regional Buses: These buses serve shorter routes within cities and regions. They are ideal for reaching suburban and rural destinations.

Advantages:
- Coverage: Reach destinations not accessible by train.
- Frequency: Regular services, especially on popular routes.
- Affordability: Often cheaper than train travel.

Tickets:
- Purchasing: Tickets can be bought online, at bus stations, or directly from the driver (for local buses). Advance booking is recommended for long-distance travel.
- Discounts: Available for students, seniors, and children.

By Car

Overview:

Renting a car in Portugal provides the ultimate freedom and flexibility, allowing you to explore at your own pace. This is especially beneficial for visiting remote areas, scenic routes, and smaller towns.

Rental Information:

- Rental Companies: Major international and local rental companies operate throughout Portugal, including at airports and in city centers.
- Requirements: You need a valid driver's license (an International Driving Permit may be required for non-EU visitors), a credit card, and be at least 21 years old (age requirements may vary by rental company).

Driving in Portugal:

- Roads: Portugal has a well-maintained road network, including highways (Autoestradas), regional roads, and scenic byways. Highways often have tolls, payable manually or via electronic toll systems.
- Fuel: Gas stations are plentiful, especially along major routes. Fuel prices are comparable to other Western European countries.
- Parking: In cities, parking can be challenging. Look for designated parking areas, and be aware of parking restrictions and fees.

Advantages:

- Flexibility: Travel on your own schedule and reach off-the-beaten-path destinations.
- Convenience: Ideal for families and groups with luggage.
- Exploration: Access to remote beaches, mountains, and countryside.

Tips for Driving:

- Navigation: Use GPS or a reliable map app. Road signs are generally clear and in Portuguese.
- Tolls: Consider renting an electronic toll device (Via Verde) for hassle-free toll payments.
- Safety: Adhere to speed limits, which are 50 km/h in urban areas, 90 km/h on rural roads, and 120 km/h on highways.

Whether you choose to travel by train, bus, or car, getting around Portugal is relatively easy and efficient. Trains offer comfort and scenic views for long-distance travel, buses provide extensive coverage and affordability, and renting a car gives you the freedom to explore at your own pace. By understanding the advantages and practicalities of each mode of transportation, you can make the best choice for your travel itinerary and enjoy all that Portugal has to offer.

Safety Tips and Emergency Contacts

Traveling to Portugal is generally safe and enjoyable, but like any destination, it's important to be aware of safety precautions and have access to emergency contacts. Here are some essential safety tips and important contact information to ensure a secure and worry-free trip.

Safety Tips

General Safety

1. Stay Aware of Your Surroundings:
- Always be mindful of your surroundings, especially in crowded places like markets, tourist attractions, and public transport.
- Keep an eye on your belongings to avoid pickpocketing, which can happen in busy areas.

2. Secure Your Valuables:

- Use a money belt or hidden pouch to store important documents, cash, and credit cards.
- Leave expensive jewelry and unnecessary valuables at your accommodation.

3. Avoid Risky Areas:

- While Portugal is safe, avoid poorly lit or deserted areas, particularly at night.
- Stick to well-populated and well-lit streets and use reputable transportation services.

Health and Wellness

4. Stay Hydrated:

- Portugal's climate can be hot, especially in the summer. Drink plenty of water to stay hydrated.

- Carry a reusable water bottle and refill it throughout the day.

5. Sun Protection:

- Use sunscreen, wear a hat, and sunglasses to protect yourself from the sun.
- Seek shade during the peak sun hours (11 AM to 3 PM).

6. Food and Water Safety:

- Tap water is generally safe to drink, but if you prefer, bottled water is readily available.
- Enjoy local cuisine, but be cautious with street food and ensure it's from a reputable vendor.

Transportation Safety

7. Road Safety:

- If renting a car, always wear your seatbelt and adhere to local traffic laws.

- Avoid driving under the influence of alcohol. Portugal has strict DUI laws.

8. Public Transportation:

- Use official and licensed taxi services or ride-sharing apps like Uber.
- On public transport, keep your bags close and be cautious of pickpockets.

Personal Safety

9. Emergency Situations:

- Familiarize yourself with emergency exits and procedures at your accommodation.
- Have a basic understanding of Portuguese emergency numbers and how to reach them.

10. Stay Connected:

- Keep your mobile phone charged and have a local SIM card or international plan for communication.
- Share your travel itinerary with a trusted friend or family member.

Emergency Contacts

General Emergency Number

112: The universal emergency number in Portugal for police, fire, and medical emergencies.

Police

Polícia de Segurança Pública (PSP):
- Responsible for urban areas and cities.
- Dial 112 for immediate assistance or visit the nearest police station.

GNR (Guarda Nacional Republicana):

- Handles rural areas and smaller towns.

- Dial 112 for emergencies or visit a local GNR post.

Medical Services

Hospitals and Clinics:

- Public hospitals provide emergency care. EU citizens can use their European Health Insurance Card (EHIC).

- Private hospitals and clinics are also available; ensure you have travel insurance that covers medical expenses.

Pharmacies (Farmácias):

- Open during regular business hours, with some open 24/7. Look for the green cross symbol.

- Pharmacists can provide advice and medication for minor health issues.

Consular Services

Embassies and Consulates:

- In case of lost passports or other consular emergencies, contact your country's embassy or consulate in Portugal.
- Most embassies are located in Lisbon, with consulates in other major cities like Porto and Faro.

Examples:

- US Embassy in Lisbon: Avenida das Forças Armadas, 1600-081 Lisbon. Phone: +351 21 727 3300
- UK Embassy in Lisbon: Rua de São Bernardo 33, 1249-082 Lisbon. Phone: +351 21 392 4000

Tourist Assistance

Tourist Police:

- Specialized units in major tourist areas, providing assistance and information to visitors.

- In Lisbon, the Tourist Police station is located near Rossio Square.

Tourist Information Centers:

- Available in major cities and tourist areas, offering maps, guides, and advice.

While Portugal is a safe and welcoming destination, staying informed about potential risks and having access to emergency contacts can enhance your travel experience. By following these safety tips and knowing who to contact in case of an emergency, you can enjoy a secure and memorable trip to Portugal.

Chapter 9

Day Trips and Excursions

Portugal's allure extends far beyond its bustling cities and picturesque coastlines. The country is brimming with charming towns, historic sites, and breathtaking natural landscapes, all within easy reach of major urban centers. Chapter 9 delves into the myriad of day trips and excursions that allow travelers to explore Portugal's rich cultural heritage and stunning scenery. Whether you're based in Lisbon, Porto, or another city, this chapter will guide you to nearby gems that promise to enhance your Portuguese adventure. From the fairytale palaces of Sintra and the wine estates of the Douro Valley to the medieval streets of Óbidos and the pristine beaches of the Algarve, discover the diverse experiences that await just a short journey away. Join us as we uncover the best day trips and excursions to help you make the most of your time in this captivating country.

Discovering Nearby Islands and Towns

While Portugal's mainland offers a wealth of attractions, its nearby islands and lesser-known towns present even more opportunities for exploration and discovery. These destinations provide a delightful mix of natural beauty, historical charm, and cultural richness. Here's a guide to some of the most captivating nearby islands and towns that you should consider adding to your itinerary.

Nearby Islands

Madeira

Overview:

- Madeira, known as the "Pearl of the Atlantic," is an archipelago renowned for its stunning landscapes, lush vegetation, and mild climate. It's a paradise for nature lovers and adventure seekers alike.

Key Attractions:
- Funchal: The capital city, with its charming old town, vibrant markets, and beautiful botanical gardens.
- Levada Walks: Explore the island's extensive network of irrigation channels through scenic hiking trails.
- Pico Ruivo: The highest peak on the island, offering breathtaking views and challenging hikes.

Activities:
- Whale and dolphin watching.
- Wine tasting tours, particularly Madeira wine.
- Exploring Laurisilva Forest, a UNESCO World Heritage site.

Azores

Overview:

- The Azores archipelago, located in the mid-Atlantic, consists of nine islands, each with unique landscapes ranging from volcanic craters to lush pastures and dramatic coastlines.

Key Attractions:

- São Miguel: Known for its geothermal hot springs, lakes such as Lagoa do Fogo and Sete Cidades, and the bustling city of Ponta Delgada.
- Pico Island: Famous for its imposing volcano, Mount Pico, the highest peak in Portugal.
- Terceira: Home to the UNESCO-listed Angra do Heroísmo and vibrant cultural festivals.

Activities:

- Hiking and trekking through stunning natural parks.

- Diving and snorkeling in crystal-clear waters.

- Whale watching and sailing adventures.

Nearby Towns

Sintra

Overview:

- Located just a short train ride from Lisbon, Sintra is a fairytale town nestled in the hills of the Serra de Sintra. It's famous for its whimsical palaces, lush gardens, and historic estates.

Key Attractions:

- Pena Palace: A colorful and eclectic palace perched on a hilltop, offering stunning views and fascinating architectural styles.

- Quinta da Regaleira: A mystical estate featuring underground tunnels, enchanting gardens, and a romantic palace.
- Moorish Castle: Ruins of a medieval castle with panoramic views of Sintra and the surrounding landscape.

Activities:

- Exploring the historic center with its narrow streets and traditional shops.
- Hiking in the Sintra-Cascais Natural Park.
- Visiting the Convent of the Capuchos, a humble and serene Franciscan convent.

Óbidos

Overview:

- Óbidos is a beautifully preserved medieval town known for its charming streets, historic buildings, and vibrant cultural scene. It's an easy day trip from Lisbon and a favorite among history enthusiasts.

Key Attractions:
- Óbidos Castle: A well-preserved castle that now functions as a luxurious pousada (historic hotel).
- Santa Maria Church: A beautiful church with stunning azulejos (traditional blue and white tiles).
- Livraria de Santiago: A unique bookstore set in a historic church.

Activities:
- Walking along the town's medieval walls for stunning views.
- Sampling the local cherry liqueur, Ginja de Óbidos.
- Attending one of the town's many festivals, such as the Medieval Market or the International Chocolate Festival.

Évora

Overview:

- Évora, a UNESCO World Heritage site, is located in the heart of the Alentejo region. This ancient city is rich in Roman history, Gothic architecture, and a unique blend of cultures.

Key Attractions:

- Temple of Diana: A remarkably preserved Roman temple dating back to the 1st century AD.
- Évora Cathedral: A stunning Gothic cathedral offering panoramic views from its roof.
- Chapel of Bones (Capela dos Ossos): A macabre yet fascinating chapel decorated with human bones.

Activities:

- Exploring the narrow streets and whitewashed houses of the historic center.

- Visiting the Évora Museum to learn about the region's history and culture.
- Tasting regional delicacies, such as Alentejo bread and wines.

Exploring Portugal's nearby islands and towns allows you to experience the country's diverse landscapes, rich history, and vibrant cultures beyond the well-trodden paths of its major cities. From the natural wonders of Madeira and the Azores to the historic charm of Sintra, Óbidos, and Évora, these destinations offer unique experiences that enhance your Portuguese adventure. Whether you're seeking adventure, tranquility, or a deep dive into history, these nearby islands and towns have something special to offer every traveler.

Wine Tasting Tours and Vineyard Visits

Portugal is renowned for its rich winemaking traditions and diverse wine regions, each offering unique flavors and experiences. Whether you're a seasoned oenophile or a casual wine lover, exploring Portugal's vineyards and indulging in wine-tasting tours is a must. From the world-famous Port wine of the Douro Valley to the crisp Vinho Verde of the Minho region, here's a guide to some of the best wine-tasting tours and vineyard visits in Portugal.

Douro Valley

Overview:

- The Douro Valley is one of the oldest demarcated wine regions in the world and a UNESCO World Heritage site. It is famous for its terraced vineyards, stunning landscapes, and production of Port wine.

Key Vineyards and Wineries:

1. Quinta do Crasto
- Overview: A historic estate offering a range of wine-tasting experiences, including Port and table wines.
- Highlights: Breathtaking views of the Douro River, vineyard tours, and tastings of premium wines.

2. Quinta da Pacheca
- Overview: One of the most iconic estates in the Douro Valley, known for its traditional and innovative wines.
- Highlights: Wine tastings, guided tours of the vineyard and cellar, and dining at the on-site restaurant with wine pairings.

3. Quinta do Vallado
- Overview: A 300-year-old winery that combines traditional winemaking techniques with modern facilities.

- Highlights: Tour of the modern winery, tastings of award-winning wines, and accommodation in a boutique hotel.

Alentejo

Overview:

- The Alentejo region, located in the heart of Portugal, is known for its vast plains, cork oak forests, and full-bodied red wines. The region's warm climate and diverse soil types contribute to its distinctive wine profile.

Key Vineyards and Wineries:

1. Herdade do Esporão
- Overview: A leading winery in Alentejo, offering a comprehensive wine tourism experience.
- Highlights: Guided tours of the vineyards and cellars, wine and olive oil tastings, and gourmet meals at the winery's restaurant.

2. Adega da Cartuxa

- Overview: A historic winery located near Évora, known for its high-quality wines and commitment to sustainability.

- Highlights: Tastings of renowned wines like Pêra-Manca, tours of the cellar, and visits to the Ecotourism Centre.

3. Herdade dos Grous

- Overview: A picturesque estate offering a blend of wine tourism and rural charm.

- Highlights: Vineyard tours, wine tastings, horseback riding, and staying at the country house.

Vinho Verde Region

Overview:

- The Vinho Verde region, located in the northwest of Portugal, is famous for its young, fresh, and slightly effervescent wines. The region's cool and rainy climate is ideal for producing these unique wines.

Key Vineyards and Wineries:

1. Quinta de Soalheiro
- Overview: A pioneering winery in the Vinho Verde region, known for its high-quality Alvarinho wines.
- Highlights: Guided tours of the vineyards, tastings of various Alvarinho wines, and visits to the winery's facilities.

2. Adega de Monção
- Overview: A cooperative winery producing some of the best Vinho Verde wines.
- Highlights: Tastings of a variety of Vinho Verde wines, tours of the production facilities, and a visit to the wine shop.

3. Quinta da Aveleda

- Overview: A historic family estate known for its beautiful gardens and exceptional wines.
- Highlights: Garden tours, wine tastings, and exploring the historic winery.

Bairrada

Overview:

- The Bairrada region, located in central Portugal, is famous for its sparkling wines and robust red wines made from the Baga grape. The region's proximity to the Atlantic Ocean influences its unique wine characteristics.

Key Vineyards and Wineries:

1. Caves São João
- Overview: A historic winery producing some of the finest sparkling wines in Portugal.

- Highlights: Tours of the extensive cellars, tastings of sparkling wines, and visits to the wine museum.

2. Adega Luís Pato
- Overview: A leading winery in the Bairrada region, known for its innovative approach to winemaking.
- Highlights: Tastings of wines made from the Baga grape, vineyard tours, and insights into modern winemaking techniques.

3. Quinta das Bágeiras
- Overview: A family-run estate producing traditional Bairrada wines.
- Highlights: Tastings of red, white, and sparkling wines, vineyard visits, and learning about traditional production methods.

Wine-tasting tours and vineyard visits in Portugal offer a delightful blend of scenic beauty, rich history, and exceptional wines. Whether you're exploring the terraced vineyards of the Douro Valley, the expansive plains of Alentejo, the lush landscapes of the Vinho Verde region, or the sparkling wine cellars of Bairrada, each wine region provides a unique and memorable experience. Indulge in the diverse flavors and traditions of Portuguese wines, and immerse yourself in the vibrant culture and hospitality of the country's renowned wine estates.

Cultural Tours and Local Experiences

Exploring Portugal's rich cultural tapestry through immersive tours and local experiences offers travelers a deeper understanding of the country's heritage, traditions, and way of life. From historical walking tours and culinary adventures to artisan workshops and music performances, there are countless ways to engage with Portugal's vibrant culture. Here are some of the best cultural tours and local experiences to consider during your visit.

Historical and Walking Tours

Lisbon

1. Alfama and Mouraria Walking Tour
- Overview: Discover the oldest neighborhoods of Lisbon, rich in history and character.
- Highlights: Explore narrow streets, traditional Fado houses, historic churches, and viewpoints offering stunning vistas of the city.

2. Belem Tour
- Overview: Dive into Portugal's Age of Discoveries in the historic Belem district.
- Highlights: Visit iconic sites like the Belem Tower, Jeronimos Monastery, and the Monument to the Discoveries. Don't forget to sample the famous Pastéis de Belém.

Porto

1. Ribeira and Miragaia Walking Tour
- Overview: Stroll through Porto's historic riverside districts.
- Highlights: Admire the colorful buildings, visit the Bolsa Palace, and enjoy the views from the Dom Luís I Bridge.

2. Porto Wine Cellar Tour
- Overview: Learn about the history of Port wine in Vila Nova de Gaia.
- Highlights: Guided tours of historic wine cellars, tastings of different Port varieties, and insights into the wine-making process.

Sintra

1. Sintra Romantic Tour

- Overview: Explore the fairytale palaces and gardens of Sintra.

- Highlights: Visit Pena Palace, Quinta da Regaleira, and Monserrate Palace, and wander through lush, romantic gardens.

Culinary Tours and Experiences

Lisbon

1. Lisbon Food and Wine Tour

- Overview: A guided tour through Lisbon's culinary hotspots.

- Highlights: Sample traditional dishes like Bacalhau à Brás, taste local wines, and visit food markets such as Mercado da Ribeira.

2. Cooking Class with a Local Chef

- Overview: Learn to cook traditional Portuguese dishes with a local chef.
- Highlights: Hands-on cooking experience, tasting your own creations, and taking home recipes to share with friends and family.

Porto

1. Porto Food Tour
- Overview: Discover Porto's culinary delights on a guided tour.
- Highlights: Taste regional specialties like Francesinha, visit local bakeries, and enjoy Port wine pairings.

2. Wine and Cheese Pairing Experience
- Overview: A sensory journey through Portuguese wine and cheese.
- Highlights: Guided tastings of local wines paired with artisanal cheeses, held in charming wine bars or cellars.

Artisan Workshops and Handicrafts

Lisbon

1. Azulejos Tile Painting Workshop
- Overview: Learn the art of traditional Portuguese tile painting.
- Highlights: Hands-on experience creating your own azulejo tile, guided by a local artisan.

2. Portuguese Pottery Workshop
- Overview: Discover the techniques behind traditional Portuguese ceramics.
- Highlights: Craft and decorate your own pottery piece under the guidance of skilled artisans.

Porto

1. Filigree Jewelry Workshop

- Overview: Explore the intricate art of Portuguese filigree jewelry making.
- Highlights: Create your own piece of jewelry, learning from experienced craftsmen in the heart of Porto.

2. Leather Craft Workshop

- Overview: Learn the craft of traditional Portuguese leatherwork.
- Highlights: Design and create your own leather accessory with the help of local artisans.

Music and Dance Experiences

Lisbon

1. Fado Night

- Overview: Experience the soulful sounds of traditional Fado music in its birthplace.

- Highlights: Enjoy live performances in historic Fado houses in Alfama and Bairro Alto, accompanied by traditional Portuguese cuisine.

2. Folk Dance Workshop
- Overview: Learn traditional Portuguese folk dances.
- Highlights: Interactive dance sessions with professional instructors, experiencing the rhythms and movements of regional dances.

Porto

1. Casa da Música Tour
- Overview: Explore Porto's iconic modern music venue.
- Highlights: Guided tours of the concert hall, learning about its architecture and the diverse musical events it hosts.

2. Fado Concert in Porto
- Overview: Enjoy an intimate Fado performance in Porto.

- Highlights: Authentic Fado music in cozy venues, often accompanied by regional dishes and wine.

Festivals and Cultural Events

Lisbon

1. Lisbon Carnival
- Overview: Join in the colorful celebrations of Lisbon's Carnival.
- Highlights: Parades, street parties, and traditional music and dance performances.

2. Saint Anthony's Festival
- Overview: Celebrate Lisbon's patron saint with locals.
- Highlights: Street decorations, sardine barbecues, and traditional music and dancing.

Porto

1. São João Festival

- Overview: Experience Porto's largest annual festival.

- Highlights: Fireworks, street parties, traditional music, and the unique tradition of hitting people with plastic hammers.

2. Porto Wine Festival

- Overview: Celebrate Porto's wine heritage.

- Highlights: Wine tastings, vineyard tours, and cultural events dedicated to Port wine.

Engaging in cultural tours and local experiences in Portugal offers a rich and immersive way to connect with the country's heritage and traditions. From exploring historic neighborhoods and savoring regional cuisines to participating in artisan workshops and enjoying live music, these experiences provide a deeper appreciation of Portugal's vibrant culture. Embrace the opportunity to interact with locals, learn traditional crafts, and celebrate festivals, making your visit to Portugal truly unforgettable.

Chapter 10

Language and Communication

Navigating a new country is made richer and more rewarding when you can connect with its people through their language. Chapter 10 of our Portugal travel guide delves into the essentials of language and communication, providing you with the tools to enhance your interactions and deepen your understanding of Portuguese culture.

In this chapter, we will explore the Portuguese language, offering key phrases and expressions to help you navigate everyday situations, from ordering food to asking for directions. We'll also discuss the nuances of local dialects and the importance of body language in communication. Additionally, this chapter provides insights into the Portuguese people's communication styles, helping you engage more effectively and respectfully with locals. Whether you are a seasoned linguist or a beginner eager to learn, this chapter will equip you with the knowledge and confidence to communicate comfortably during your travels in Portugal.

Useful Portuguese Phrases and Expressions

Learning a few key Portuguese phrases and expressions can greatly enhance your travel experience in Portugal. While many locals, especially in tourist areas, speak English, making an effort to communicate in Portuguese will be appreciated and can open doors to more authentic interactions. Here are some essential phrases and expressions to help you navigate your journey.

Basic Greetings and Politeness

Hello / Hi: Olá

Good morning: Bom dia

Good afternoon: Boa tarde

Good evening / Good night: Boa noite

Goodbye: Adeus

See you later: Até logo

Please: Por favor

Thank you: Obrigado (if you're male) / Obrigada (if you're female)

You're welcome: De nada

Yes: Sim

No: Não

Excuse me / Sorry: Desculpe

Introductions

What is your name?: Como se chama?

My name is...: Chamo-me...

Nice to meet you: Prazer em conhecê-lo (if you're speaking to a male) / Prazer em conhecê-la (if you're speaking to a female)

How are you?: Como está?

I'm fine, thank you: Estou bem, obrigado (if you're male) / Estou bem, obrigada (if you're female)

Asking for Directions

Where is...?: Onde fica...?

How do I get to...?: Como chego a...?

Left: Esquerda

Right: Direita

Straight ahead: Em frente

Near: Perto

Far: Longe

Is it far?: É longe?

Can you help me?: Pode ajudar-me?

Dining Out

Menu: Ementa / Cardápio

Waiter / Waitress: Empregado / Empregada

I would like...: Gostaria de...

What do you recommend?: O que recomenda?

Water: Água

Wine: Vinho

Beer: Cerveja

Coffee: Café

The bill, please: A conta, por favor

Delicious: Delicioso

I'm allergic to...: Sou alérgico a... (if you're male) / Sou alérgica a... (if you're female)

Shopping and Services

How much does it cost?: Quanto custa?

I would like to buy...: Gostaria de comprar...

Do you have...?: Tem...?

Where can I find...?: Onde posso encontrar...?

Open: Aberto

Closed: Fechado

What time do you open/close?: A que horas abre / fecha?

Emergencies

Help!: Socorro!

I need a doctor: Preciso de um médico

Call the police: Chame a polícia

I'm lost: Estou perdido (if you're male) / Estou perdida (if you're female)

I've lost my passport: Perdi o meu passaporte

Useful Expressions

Can you speak English?: Fala inglês?

I don't understand: Não entendo

Can you repeat that?: Pode repetir?

Can you speak more slowly?: Pode falar mais devagar?

What does this mean?: O que significa isto?

Do you have Wi-Fi?: Tem Wi-Fi?

What is the Wi-Fi password?: Qual é a senha do Wi-Fi?

Mastering a few Portuguese phrases can significantly enhance your travel experience, helping you navigate daily interactions and showing locals that you appreciate their culture. Whether you're greeting someone, ordering a meal, or asking for directions, these essential expressions will make your journey smoother and more enjoyable. Practice these phrases before your trip, and don't be afraid to use them— most locals will appreciate your effort and respond warmly.

Etiquette and Cultural Norms

Understanding and respecting the cultural norms and etiquette of Portugal can greatly enhance your travel experience and help you connect more deeply with the local people. Here are some key aspects of Portuguese etiquette and cultural norms that you should be aware of during your visit.

Greetings and Social Interactions

Formal Greetings:
- Portuguese people often greet each other with a handshake. This is common in both formal and informal settings. For a more formal introduction, use titles such as

"Senhor" (Mr.) or "Senhora" (Mrs.) followed by the person's last name.

Informal Greetings:

- Among friends and family, it's common to greet with a hug and two kisses on the cheeks, starting with the right cheek. This is typical between women or between a man and a woman, but less common between men.

Common Phrases:

- Use polite expressions like "Bom dia" (Good morning), "Boa tarde" (Good afternoon), and "Boa noite" (Good evening) when greeting people. Saying "Por favor" (Please) and "Obrigado/Obrigada" (Thank you) is also very important.

Dining Etiquette

Table Manners:

- Wait to be invited to sit down at the table. The host usually indicates where guests should sit.
- Keep your hands visible but do not rest your elbows on the table.
- Use utensils rather than eating with your hands, even for foods like fruit.

Ordering and Eating:

- It's polite to wait for everyone to be served before you start eating.
- When you're finished eating, place your knife and fork parallel on your plate.

Paying the Bill:

- In restaurants, it's customary to signal for the bill by making a written gesture or saying "A conta, por favor" (The bill, please).

- Tipping is appreciated but not obligatory. Leaving a 5-10% tip for good service is common, or rounding up the bill.

Dress Code

General Attire:

- Dress smartly, especially in urban areas. Portuguese people tend to dress more formally compared to other European countries.
- For business meetings or formal events, men usually wear suits and ties, while women wear dresses or smart suits.

Beachwear:

- Swimwear is appropriate at the beach or pool, but not in town or restaurants. Make sure to cover up when leaving beach areas.

Social Norms

Punctuality:

- While punctuality is appreciated, social events and casual gatherings tend to have a more relaxed attitude towards time. However, for business meetings and formal appointments, being on time is important.

Personal Space:

- Portuguese people value personal space and may stand closer during conversations than people in some other cultures. Light physical contacts, such as a pat on the back or a touch on the arm, is common.

Conversations:

- Engage in friendly small talk before jumping into serious discussions. Topics like family, food, and sports (especially football) are good conversation starters.
- Avoid controversial topics such as politics or religion unless you know the person well.

Quietness:

- Speak in moderate tones in public places. Loud behavior is generally frowned upon.
- On public transport, it's polite to give up your seat for the elderly, pregnant women, or those with disabilities.

Respect for Tradition:

- Respecting local traditions and customs is important. For instance, during religious festivals or processions, observe respectfully and follow the lead of locals.

Business Etiquette

Meetings:

- Arrange meetings in advance and confirm them a day or two before. Business cards are commonly exchanged.

- Be prepared for small talk before the actual business discussion starts. Building personal relationships is key in Portuguese business culture.

Negotiations:
- Decisions are often made at the top level. Be patient, as decision-making can take time.
- A direct approach is valued, but politeness and diplomacy are essential.

By understanding and respecting Portuguese etiquette and cultural norms, you can ensure a more pleasant and meaningful interaction with locals during your visit. Embrace the opportunity to learn from the rich cultural heritage of Portugal, and you'll find that your efforts to engage respectfully will be warmly received. Whether you're dining out, navigating social situations, or conducting business, these guidelines will help you navigate Portuguese society with ease and respect.

Chapter 11

Shopping Guide

Welcome to Chapter 11 of your Portugal travel guide, where we delve into the vibrant and diverse world of shopping in this enchanting country. From bustling markets brimming with local produce and traditional crafts to chic boutiques and modern shopping malls, Portugal offers a rich tapestry of shopping experiences that cater to every taste and budget.

In this chapter, we will explore the best shopping destinations across Portugal, highlighting unique souvenirs and must-have items that capture the essence of Portuguese culture. Whether you are on the hunt for handcrafted ceramics, exquisite embroidery, or world-renowned Port wine, our comprehensive shopping guide will help you discover treasures that make perfect mementos for your trip.

We'll also provide practical tips on navigating local markets, understanding pricing and bargaining practices, and even shopping tax-free. By the end of this chapter, you'll be well-equipped to enjoy the best of Portuguese shopping, bringing home not just souvenirs, but stories and memories of your journey.

Souvenirs and Local Products

When visiting Portugal, bringing back a piece of the country's rich culture and heritage through souvenirs and local products can make your trip even more memorable. From traditional handicrafts to delectable culinary treats, here are some of the best souvenirs and local products to consider:

Handcrafted Items

1. Azulejos (Tiles):

- Overview: Portugal is famous for its beautiful ceramic tiles, known as azulejos. These hand-painted tiles often depict intricate patterns, historical scenes, or floral designs.
- Where to Buy: Look for azulejos in specialized tile shops, local markets, and gift shops, especially in Lisbon and Porto.

2. Portuguese Pottery:

- Overview: Traditional Portuguese pottery includes colorful bowls, plates, and vases, often featuring rustic designs and vibrant colors.
- Where to Buy: Visit regions like Alentejo and the town of Caldas da Rainha for authentic pottery pieces.

3. Cork Products:

- Overview: Portugal is the world's largest producer of cork, and you can find a variety of cork products, including bags, wallets, hats, and even shoes.
- Where to Buy: Cork shops are widespread, especially in Lisbon, Porto, and the Algarve region.

4. Filigree Jewelry:

- Overview: Portuguese filigree is a delicate jewelry technique using fine gold or silver threads to create intricate designs. Traditional pieces often include earrings, necklaces, and brooches.
- Where to Buy: The best filigree jewelry can be found in the northern regions, particularly in Porto and Viana do Castelo.

Culinary Delights

1. Port Wine:

- Overview: No visit to Portugal is complete without sampling Port wine. This fortified wine comes in several varieties, including ruby, tawny, and vintage.
- Where to Buy: Purchase Port wine from wine cellars in Vila Nova de Gaia, across the river from Porto, or at specialized wine shops.

2. Olive Oil:

- Overview: Portuguese olive oil is renowned for its high quality and rich flavor. Many local producers offer extra virgin olive oil made from traditional methods.
- Where to Buy: Look for olive oil in gourmet shops, markets, and directly from producers in regions like Alentejo and the Douro Valley.

3. Pastéis de Nata (Custard Tarts):

- Overview: These delicious custard tarts are a staple of Portuguese pastry. While they are best enjoyed fresh, many shops sell boxed versions to take home.
- Where to Buy: The best pastéis de nata can be found in Lisbon, particularly at Pastéis de Belém.

4. Portuguese Cheese:

- Overview: Portugal produces a variety of unique cheeses, such as Queijo da Serra, Azeitão, and São Jorge.

- Where to Buy: Cheese shops, markets, and gourmet food stores throughout the country.

Textiles and Embroidery

1. Arraiolos Rugs:
- Overview: These hand-embroidered woolen rugs originate from the town of Arraiolos and feature intricate geometric patterns.
- Where to Buy: Visit Arraiolos or specialized rug shops in major cities.

2. Embroidery:
- Overview: Madeira and mainland Portugal are known for exquisite hand-embroidered linens, including tablecloths, napkins, and bed linens.
- Where to Buy: Look for embroidery in markets, craft shops, and directly from artisans in Madeira and the northern regions.

Local Art and Crafts

1. Barcelos Rooster:

- Overview: The colorful rooster of Barcelos is a symbol of Portugal and represents good luck. These ceramic roosters are available in various sizes and designs.
- Where to Buy: Souvenir shops and markets across Portugal, especially in Barcelos.

2. Traditional Music Instruments:

- Overview: Bring home a piece of Portugal's musical heritage with traditional instruments like the Portuguese guitar, used in Fado music.
- Where to Buy: Music stores and specialty shops in Lisbon and Porto.

Practical Tips for Shopping

1. Markets and Fairs:

- Visiting local markets and fairs is a great way to find unique souvenirs and interact with local artisans. Notable markets include the Feira da Ladra in Lisbon and Mercado do Bolhão in Porto.

2. Bargaining:

- Bargaining is not common in regular shops but may be acceptable in markets and with street vendors. Always negotiate politely and be prepared to accept the initial price if bargaining is not customary.

3. Tax-Free Shopping:

- Non-EU residents can claim a VAT refund on purchases over a certain amount. Look for shops displaying the "Tax-Free Shopping" sign and keep your receipts to claim your refund at the airport before departure.

Bringing home a souvenir from Portugal is more than just purchasing an item; it's about capturing the essence of the country's culture, craftsmanship, and culinary delights. Whether you choose handcrafted ceramics, exquisite jewelry, or delectable Port wine, these souvenirs will serve as cherished reminders of your Portuguese adventure. Happy shopping!

Markets and Shopping Districts

Exploring the markets and shopping districts of Portugal is a delightful way to immerse yourself in the local culture, discover unique treasures, and experience the vibrant atmosphere of Portuguese cities. From bustling urban markets to charming neighborhood boutiques, here are some of the best places to shop in Portugal.

Lisbon

1. Feira da Ladra (Thieves Market):

- Overview: Lisbon's most famous flea market, is held every Tuesday and Saturday in the Alfama district.

- What to Find: Antiques, vintage items, second-hand goods, handmade crafts, and souvenirs.

- Tip: Arrive early to find the best deals and explore the nearby sights of Alfama.

2. Mercado da Ribeira (Time Out Market):

- Overview: A historic market hall in Cais do Sodré, transformed into a modern food and cultural market.

- What to Find: Gourmet food stalls, local delicacies, fresh produce, artisanal products, and dining options.

- Tip: Visit for a meal and sample dishes from some of Lisbon's top chefs.

3. Chiado and Baixa Districts:

- Overview: Central Lisbon's prime shopping areas, are known for their elegant streets and historic charm.

- What to Find: International brands, high-end boutiques, bookstores, and traditional shops.
- Tip: Don't miss Livraria Bertrand, the world's oldest operating bookstore, and Conserveira de Lisboa for Portuguese canned fish.

Porto

1. Mercado do Bolhão:
- Overview: Porto's iconic market, located in the city center, is known for its lively atmosphere and fresh produce.
- What to Find: Fresh seafood, local cheeses, cured meats, fruits, vegetables, and flowers.
- Tip: Visit in the morning for the freshest produce and to experience the bustling market at its peak.

2. Rua de Santa Catarina:
- Overview: Porto's main shopping street, stretches through the city center.

- What to Find: Major retail chains, department stores, cafes, and traditional shops.
- Tip: Enjoy a coffee at the historic Café Majestic, a beautifully ornate café on Rua de Santa Catarina.

3. Mercado Ferreira Borges:
- Overview: A striking iron market hall near the Ribeira district, now a cultural and entertainment venue.
- What to Find: Art exhibitions, cultural events, restaurants, and bars.
- Tip: Check out the event schedule for live music, exhibitions, and other cultural activities.

Algarve

1. Mercado Municipal de Loulé:
- Overview: A vibrant market in the town of Loulé, known for its Moorish-style architecture.

- What to Find: Fresh seafood, local produce, regional specialties, crafts, and textiles.
- Tip: Visit on Saturdays for the weekly farmers' market and a wider selection of goods.

2. Avenida da Liberdade, Faro:
- Overview: A central shopping street in Faro, the capital of the Algarve region.
- What to Find: Fashion boutiques, souvenir shops, jewelry stores, and cafes.
- Tip: Stroll along the nearby marina for beautiful views and additional shopping options.

Madeira

1. Mercado dos Lavradores (Farmers' Market):
- Overview: Funchal's central market, offers a colorful array of local produce and crafts.

- What to Find: Exotic fruits, fresh fish, flowers, Madeira wine, and artisanal products.

- Tip: Visit the fish market section to see the impressive displays of local catches, including the famous black scabbardfish.

2. Rua Fernão de Ornelas:

- Overview: One of Funchal's main shopping streets, lined with shops and cafes.

- What to Find: Clothing, accessories, souvenirs, and local delicacies.

- Tip: Explore the nearby Funchal Old Town for more shopping and dining options in a historic setting.

Alentejo

1. Évora Market:

- Overview: A bustling market in the historic city of Évora, held in the city center.

- What to Find: Fresh produce, local meats, cheeses, olive oil, and crafts.

- Tip: Combine your market visit with a tour of Évora's UNESCO-listed historic sites.

2. Arraiolos:

- Overview: A town famous for its handmade embroidered rugs.

- What to Find: Beautifully crafted Arraiolos rugs, textiles, and home decor items.

- Tip: Visit local workshops to see artisans at work and learn about the rug-making process.

Azores

1. Mercado da Graça, Ponta Delgada:

- Overview: The main market in Ponta Delgada on São Miguel Island.

- What to Find: Fresh produce, local cheeses, fish, Azorean pineapples, and handmade crafts.
- Tip: Try the local cheese and Azorean pineapples for a taste of the island's unique flavors.

2. Rua da Sé, Angra do Heroísmo:
- Overview: A charming street in the historic center of Angra do Heroísmo on Terceira Island.
- What to Find: Boutique shops, local crafts, souvenirs, and traditional pastries.
- Tip: Explore the historic architecture and UNESCO World Heritage sites while shopping.

Portugal's markets and shopping districts offer a diverse and enriching shopping experience, allowing you to discover local crafts, taste regional specialties, and enjoy the vibrant atmosphere of Portuguese cities. Whether you're seeking unique souvenirs, gourmet food products, or fashionable clothing, these markets and shopping areas have something for every traveler. Happy shopping!

Printed in Great Britain
by Amazon